AMERICAN POETS PROJECT

AMERICAN POETS PROJECT

IS PUBLISHED WITH A GIFT IN MEMORY OF

James Merrill

AND SUPPORT FROM ITS FOUNDING PATRONS

Sidney J. Weinberg, Jr. Foundation

The Berkley Foundation

Richard B. Fisher and Jeanne Donovan Fisher

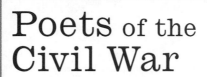

Poets of the Civil War

j. d. mcclatchy editor

AMERICAN POETS PROJECT

THE LIBRARY OF AMERICA

Design by Chip Kidd and Mark Melnick.
Frontispiece: Union soldier from Larry B. Williford, Portsmouth, VA

Library of Congress Cataloging-in-Publication Data:
Poets of the Civil War / J. D. McClatchy, editor.
        p. cm. — (American poets project ; 14)
    Includes bibliographical references.
    ISBN 1-931082-76-6 (alk. paper)
     1. American poetry—19th century. 2. United States—Civil War,
1861–1865—Poetry. 3. War poetry, American. I. McClatchy, J. D., 1945–
II. Series.

PS595.C55P648 2005
811'.4080358— dc22
2004061552

10 9 8 7 6 5 4 3 2 1

Poets of the Civil War

CONTENTS

INTRODUCTION

It remains the most cataclysmic and tragic event in our history. Behind the struggle, driving its purpose and passions, loomed the greatest of issues: the fate of a country and the rights of its people. Hateful decisions were at the heart of the conflict. A Northern sense of justice and a Southern sense of honor, moral principle and emotional pride, drove men to their deaths amid the terrors of war: the deafening noise, the blinding smoke, the ground slick with blood, the cries of the fallen. Over 620,000 soldiers died during those four years, nearly as many as in all of America's other wars combined.

Proud cities were put to the torch, civilian populations were brutalized, fertile countryside was reduced to wasteland. Brother fought against brother, and there was scarcely a household in the land that did not have a loss to mourn. The very names of the fearsome battles and valiant commanders ring in people's memories with the force of myth. The grandeur and pathos of the two shredded armies never fail to thrill. In the end slavery would be abolished, secession defeated, and a new nation born in fire, blood, and sorrow. And each side in the conflict would discover its tragic hero: for the South, Robert E. Lee, the model Virginia gentleman who fought for the Lost Cause with audacious skill and relentless determination; for the North, Abraham Lincoln, the martyred redeemer-president who spoke for American democracy with an eloquence unmatched in our history.

It is such stuff as epics are made on.

Yet no one great, sweeping poem—no American *Iliad* —ever emerged from this most momentous event in the lives and imaginations of Americans. All the arts, in fact, shied away. The most talented novelists of the day—from Henry James to Mark Twain to William Dean Howells— avoided the subject. Our leading painters were doing Hudson Valley scenes. Our strongest composers were studying in Europe. Many of the best poets were writing moralistic meditations on nature. Explanations have been advanced. Chief among them is that the war, with its mechanized brutality and enormity, simply overwhelmed the talents of contemporary artists to portray what was happening. (Much the same thing happened to German writers during and for some time after World War II.) By its end, the doctrine of total war was in place, the costs of which are still incomprehensible. In the major battles of the war, the carnage was staggering. At Antietam, for instance, on September 17, 1862, it is thought that as many as 6,500 soldiers were killed, making it the bloodiest day in American history, with more casualties than at Pearl Harbor or on D-Day. By the end of the war, weary soldiers were writing their names on scraps of paper and pinning them to their uniforms, so their bodies could be identified. The trenches ran with the slimy blood of the dead, over whose bodies soldiers fighting for their lives clambered, throwing their empty bayoneted rifles like spears against their enemy. Nothing had prepared our writers, for whom Sir Walter Scott was still a model, to absorb and transfigure facts like those before their eyes.

In 1861, Nathaniel Hawthorne wrote, "I apprehend that no people ever built up the skeleton of a warlike history so rapidly as we are doing. What a fine theme for a poet!" But before long, Walt Whitman, listening to the stories of wounded soldiers just back from the front, and himself one of the era's great chroniclers, realized that "the real war will never get in the books." It could be said that the best writing about the Civil War was done long after the events and was the work of historians and memoirists, just as, at the time, the most expressive views of the war and its toll (aside from the astonishing images made by such photographers as Alexander Gardner, Mathew Brady, and George S. Cook) were written by prose elegists like Lincoln in his Gettysburg Address and Second Inaugural or Whitman in his magnificent *Specimen Days*. That is true. Still, the poets of the Civil War, whether overwhelmed or partisan or detached, brought to the crisis poetry's unique ability to stir the emotions, to freeze the moment, to sweep the scene with a panoramic lens and suddenly swoop in for a close-up of suffering or courage.

Much of the poetry written during and about the war—this is true of any war—is second-rate. Newspapers of the day were filled with patriotic rant, and Unionist or Secessionist activism inspired jingoistic anthems. Even the preferred poetic style of the day—too often mere melodramatic narrative and sentimental effusion—worked against a depth equal to the events described. Still, examples of such poems—anthems and elegies, rallying cries and defenses—are included in this volume as a part of the era's literary history, the backdrop against which stronger poems are illuminated. At the other extreme from such tub-thumpers are poems that use the war as a private metaphor. Emily Dickinson, for instance, who wrote her poems in waves, one of which coincided with the war years, may have thought the war seemed remote from her Amherst bedroom. Still, reports of it overwhelmed her: "It feels a shame to be Alive – / When Men so brave – are dead –" But reports from the front never overmastered her ability to absorb facts into her own moral cosmos, as emblems of forces contending for her soul. And her take on commonplaces—say, the bold soldier who risked death, was hit, and now lies dying on the field—can be disconcerting:

> His Comrades, shifted like the Flakes
> When Gusts reverse the Snow –
> But He – was left alive Because
> Of Greediness to die –

The variety of poems in this anthology should remind its readers that *this* book, in fact, approximates the great poem—dozens of brilliant, if partial, glimpses of the war that in the end yield a devastating portrait. And they must be read aright. Poetry in the twentieth century narrowed to the increasingly oblique and intimate lyric. Great issues and events were banished from poems that now focused on the fragmented self. Psychology replaced history as a literary model. But in the mid-nineteenth century, poems were able still to engage large ideas, to count on narrative skills, to turn art's moral light on public matters and private deeds. The national crisis, played out in individual lives, came to dominate the imaginations of many of the country's most prominent poets. Emerson, Bryant, Whittier, Holmes, roused by the disgrace of slavery and the threat to the nation, all responded—and often prompted others to do the same. Longfellow's *Poems of Slavery* appeared as early as 1842. (He had been impressed by the chapter on slavery in Charles Dickens' *American Notes* and, on his voyage home from visiting the novelist, quickly wrote the poems, the stormy weather and difficult voyage reminding him of the infamous Middle Passage.)

Poetry, with its cultural authority, helped to raise the stakes and to force opinion. During the war, it helped give perspective and color to the rush of events, as after the war it helped the dazed country to understand the convulsion that had seized it and to heal its divisions. James Russell Lowell, member of a distinguished New England family, professor at Harvard and influential man of letters, was an early and ardent abolitionist. But, the war over at last, at a ceremony on July 21, 1865, to honor Harvard men who had fallen in battle, he delivered his acclaimed "Ode." The victors always have Truth on their side, and Lowell begins by claiming of his young heroes: "Those love her best who to themselves are true, / And what they dare to dream of, dare to do." But at the poem's ringing conclusion, moving beyond anger, pride, and gratitude, Lowell celebrates "the kindling continent," honors the country—the idea of a country—rescued and redemptive.

It has been suggested that if any group of poets were destined to be the true bards of the Civil War it should have been the Southern poets. Most of the war, after all, was fought in the South, and the saga of its defiance, its daring, and its defeat should have afforded its poets the material for enthralling and heartbroken poems. There are two reasons why that was not to be the case: First, before the war there was no extensive literary culture in the South. The centers of publishing, intellectual debate, and university culture were all in the North. Planters preferred telling stories to reading books, and what writers there were tended to be gentlemen amateurs. One prominent Southern writer, the prolific William Gilmore Simms, recognized that an audience consisting of "cultured gentlemen, trained in the liberal arts and in the law, who turned to literature for refreshment and relaxation" was unlikely to demand of Southern poets work of the highest order. Second, the language of most Southern poetry played to the myth its politicians had promulgated. Arrogant Billy Yanks and delusional Johnny Rebs alike were rapt by visions of themselves as right and invincible. Where the poetic diction of the North was often religious, that of the South was usually chivalrous; the one was embarked on a crusade, the other jousting in a tournament. Poems in the South—by the likes of Simms, Paul Hamilton Hayne, Margaret Junkin Preston, Francis Orray Ticknor, or Abram Joseph Ryan—rhapsodized about knights and cavaliers and paladins, terms that drew a romantic scrim over the realities. This same impulse was continued after the war with the rise of the fabled Lost Cause. As Robert Penn Warren remarked about the South in defeat, in his book *The Legacy of the Civil War*, "in the moment of death the Confederacy entered upon its immortality."

The best of the Southern poets, however, resisted all this. The Georgia poet Sidney Lanier, who had fought in the war and been captured (in prison camp he contracted the tuberculosis that eventually killed him in 1881), for the most part wrote about his experience in abstruse allegories. A better poet, often called the Poet Laureate of the Confederacy, was Henry Timrod. He too served in the militia and contracted tuberculosis. His home and possessions were lost when Sherman's army burned Columbia, and he lived in pain and poverty for just two years after the war.

His poems reflect a more somber temperament than that of his patron Simms or friend Hayne. A fervent supporter of the Southern cause but impatient with cant, he came to write of the war with some reluctance. "The lyre of Tyrtaeus is the only one to which the Public will listen," he wrote in 1861, "and over that martial instrument I have but small command." Belligerence did not lure him so much as beneficence, his vision of the South as a source of kindness and prosperity. It was not heroics but peace he championed. Though a call to arms, his "Ethnogenesis" —its title proclaiming the birth not just of a new nation but of a new race—imagines the warmth of the South, "Strange tropic warmth and hints of summer seas," as a moral force for good. His characteristic note, in a moment of triumph, is "Go forth and bid the land rejoice, / Yet not too gladly, oh my song!" His moving memorial "Lines" pays homage to "defeated valor," but with a cautious delicacy.

If, as many Unionists at the time believed, the Civil War completed the work of the Revolution, it also signaled a break with what some would see as the agrarian innocence of America's past. The Gilded Age that followed the war, an era beset with cynical corruption and greed as well as with enormous industrial advances and social change, was a new world for which few were prepared, but its harsh ironies ushered a new realism into American writing. To write frankly of episodes of the war demanded a kind of sensibility that would not emerge until later, and would not have found favor with demure readers of the day. What soldiers witnessed in combat—they called it "seeing the elephant"—writers of any age would be hard-pressed to dramatize. As would be expected, the most virulent poems urging men to fight for the cause were written by those who never saw battle. Those who themselves saw the elephant wrote by far the most detailed, detached, and least partisan poems.

Some offered eyewitness accounts. In 1862 Henry Howard Brownell wrote a poem about Admiral David Farragut's attack on New Orleans that came to Farragut's attention. The admiral then invited Brownell to accompany him on his flagship *Hartford*—which brought Brownell unexpectedly into the middle of the battle of Mobile Bay. Brownell's verse account of the day, "The Bay Fight," is as accurate as any newspaper's and much more stirring. What was wanted by other soldier-poets, though, was not accuracy but a certain kind of irony, not so much cynical as surgical. Four poets in this book—all of them saw service— exemplify a style too rare at the time. Fitz-James O'Brien, born in Ireland, was a well-known critic, playwright, and short-story writer in New York—and a regular at Pfaff's Cellar, Whitman's favorite pub—when he volunteered in the Union army. The poems he wrote during his service were published in *Harper's* and offer graphic witness to the military life. His poem "A Soldier's Letter," in an odd hexameter stanza, is decidedly melodramatic, but shows a genuine theatrical flair. In March 1862, O'Brien was shot by the enemy but managed to kill his attacker and rally his men. His wound, though, proved fatal. He was just 33 when he died. Ambrose Bierce joined the 9th Indiana Infantry in 1861, saw action at Shiloh, Murfreesboro, Chattanooga, and Franklin, and survived to have an adventurous life. His mordant take on things ("I know what uniform I wore— / O, that I knew which side I fought for!") continues to resonate.

Nathaniel Southgate Shaler, a Kentucky-born and Harvard-educated geologist whose sympathies were with the South but whose loyalty was to the North, wrote sharp-eyed poems about the war in Kentucky. After the war, he became professor of paleontology and geology at Harvard and was active in scientific research, but he was also a vivid memoirist, and his poems have the scientist's objective perspective. Yet, as William James said to Shaler's widow, his poems "all swim in that atmosphere of landscape and heroic fate, and mortal sadness in the life of man." Shaler wrote with a Tolstoyan sense of the "vast thinginess of everything," and would pause to note the width of a howitzer's bore or the scream of a wounded horse. And John W. De Forest, though recognized more for his *Miss Ravenel's Conversion*, the best novel about the war, was another such realist. As a young man he had traveled, first to Syria because of his health and later to Europe because of his curiosity, and out of his travels he wrote several books. When war was declared, he returned to his native New Haven, Connecticut, and raised a company of soldiers. He saw a good deal of action, in Louisiana and with Sheridan in the Shenandoah Valley. His experience gave the battle-pieces in his novels and poems a graphic immediacy that his contemporaries recognized at once. De Forest wrote with precision and an eerie modernity, as when he ends a sonnet from "Campaigning" this way:

> And flying from afar, the shell
> With changeful, throbbing, husky yell,
>   A demon tiger, leaping miles
> To spread his iron claws
>   And tear the bleeding files;
> While oft arose the charging cry
>   Of men who battled for a glorious cause
> And died when it was beautiful to die.

Who wrote like that until Wilfred Owen?

The two great poets of the Civil War, Walt Whitman in *Drum-Taps* (1865) and Herman Melville in *Battle-Pieces and Aspects of the War* (1866), succeeded in part because both wrote about it at some distance. Whitman's view of the battlefield was from a hospital window, the cost of war finally more important than its cause, and Melville's was abstracted, the affairs of men seen from a Hardy-esque height. At 42, Melville was too old and infirm to serve in the army, but he followed developments in the war intently —through newspapers, the *Rebellion Record*, and visits to military installations. In 1864, Massachusetts senator Charles Sumner obtained a pass for Melville so he could visit a cousin at the Virginia front, where he inspected battlefields, met with General Grant, and even went on a "scout." What he saw, what he felt, both exhilarated and terrified him—and gave him a subject for poetry as vast as the sea had been for his novels. The romance of the war, its display of sheer power, is countered by a desperate realism: "What like a bullet can undeceive!" The generous boys in happiness bred

> Went from the North and came from the South,
> With golden mottoes in the mouth,
>> To lie down midway on a bloody bed.

Though a fervent Unionist, Melville cast a cold eye on ideological distinctions:

> Warred one for Right, and one for Wrong?
> So put it; but they both were young—
> Each grape to his cluster clung,
> All their elegies are sung.

As a rule, Melville did not write with Whitman's lithe, lyrical line. His tone is granitic, metaphysical, flecked with archaisms, bookish, at times jagged or prosaic. But he was engaged in a difficult project and required a style to assail the high tragic ground. With his instinctive lust for ultimates, he is fascinated less by the fate of the individual soldier than by the impersonal, unknowable forces—what he calls "strong Necessity"—driving men to their destruction. That is one reason his poems are drawn to war's "plain mechanic power"—to ironclads, artillery, railroads:

> Deadlier, closer, calm 'mid storm;
> No passion; all went on by crank,
>> Pivot, and screw,
> And calculations of caloric.

It was this power that eventually won the malignant war of attrition. The glorious boys chewed up in it, the silent veterans standing ready, the convulsions of siege and counterattack—Melville's poems are their staging ground, and from the hill the poet watches through field glasses.

Whitman's first poems about the war were full-throated war whoops. "Beat! Beat! Drums!" is an exuberant example. But once he had had a taste of war, his poems changed. In December 1862, word came that his brother George had been wounded in the battle of Fredericksburg and Whitman set off at once for Virginia to find and care for him. George survived, and Whitman stayed on with his regiment, observing and listening. His poems, often now in the voice of a soldier recounting a moment in the maelstrom, grew more muted and precise. He soon removed to Washington and at once realized that his "harsh and superb plight" was not fervently to rally new recruits but patiently to visit the city's army hospitals and comfort the shattered young men:

> Arous'd and angry, I'd thought to beat the alarum, and urge relentless war,
> But soon my fingers fail'd me, my face droop'd and I resign'd myself,
> To sit by the wounded and soothe them, or silently watch the dead . . .

"I had never before," he wrote to his brother Jeff, "had my feelings so thoroughly and (so far) permanently absorbed, to the very roots, as by these huge swarms of dear, wounded, sick, dying boys—I get very much attached to some of them, and many of them have come to depend on seeing me, and having me sit by them a few minutes, as if for their lives." He moved through the wards, he said, "like a great wild buffalo, with much hair. Many of the soldiers are from the West, and far North, and they take to a man that has not the bleached shiny and shaved cut of the cities and the East." He tended to his darlings, his "frighten'd, shy animals" with heroic steadfastness, bringing gifts (horehound drops, tobacco, a rice pudding), running errands, helping them write home, or spending the night at a bedside, holding a statistic's hand to ease him into death. The character he made of himself he called The Wound-Dresser, a poignant admission both of his compassion for democracy's braves and of the fact that the Civil War had destroyed the visionary utopianism at the heart of his *Leaves of Grass*. The final wound he dressed was the nation's own—Lincoln's assassination. His great threnody "When Lilacs Last in the Dooryard Bloom'd" is addressed to the martyred president, but also to the country's fallen sons: ". . . I break the sprigs from the bushes, / With loaded arms I come, pouring for you, / For you and the coffins all of you O death."

When Robert E. Lee was called to testify before the Congressional Reconstruction Committee in April 1866, he was asked at the end of his appearance if he wished to say anything else. He waived the invitation and merely elaborated on an earlier answer. But when Melville wrote of the incident, in his poem "Lee in the Capitol," he could not help trying to imagine what Lee might have said if he had opened his heart. Having stated the South would not recant, but yield, his Lee goes on to urge leniency so that the wounds of the nation may not bleed again. Then the old man walks out. Watching Lee depart, Melville sees in his mind's eye that "The Past her shadow through the Future sent." And so it has been. The shadow of the Civil War continues to fall across both America's history and its promise, and the poems in this book trace the outlines of that shadow—in whose depths we still see the fallen soldier, the freed slave, all the glory and grief of those fateful years.

J. D. McClatchy
2004

WILLIAM CULLEN BRYANT | 1794–1878

The Death of Slavery

O thou great Wrong, that, through the slow-paced years,
   Didst hold thy millions fettered, and didst wield
   The scourge that drove the laborer to the field,
And turn a stony gaze on human tears,
         Thy cruel reign is o'er;
         Thy bondmen crouch no more
In terror at the menace of thine eye;
   For He who marks the bounds of guilty power,
Long-suffering, hath heard the captive's cry,
   And touched his shackles at the appointed hour,
And lo! they fall, and he whose limbs they galled
Stands in his native manhood, disenthralled.

A shout of joy from the redeemed is sent;
   Ten thousand hamlets swell the hymn of thanks;
   Our rivers roll exulting, and their banks
Send up hosannas to the firmament!
         Fields where the bondman's toil
         No more shall trench the soil,
Seem now to bask in a serener day;
   The meadow-birds sing sweeter, and the airs
Of heaven with more caressing softness play,
   Welcoming man to liberty like theirs.
A glory clothes the land from sea to sea,
For the great land and all its coasts are free.

Within that land wert thou enthroned of late,
　　And they by whom the nation's laws were made,
　　And they who filled its judgment-seats obeyed
Thy mandate, rigid as the will of Fate.
　　　　　Fierce men at thy right hand,
　　　　　With gesture of command,
Gave forth the word that none might dare gainsay;
　　And grave and reverend ones, who loved thee not,
Shrank from thy presence, and in blank dismay
　　Choked down, unuttered, the rebellious thought;
While meaner cowards, mingling with thy train,
Proved, from the book of God, thy right to reign.

Great as thou wert, and feared from shore to shore,
　　The wrath of Heaven o'ertook thee in thy pride;
　　Thou sitt'st a ghastly shadow; by thy side
Thy once strong arms hang nerveless evermore.
　　　　　And they who quailed but now
　　　　　Before thy lowering brow,
Devote thy memory to scorn and shame,
　　And scoff at the pale, powerless thing thou art.
And they who ruled in thine imperial name,
　　Subdued, and standing sullenly apart,
Scowl at the hands that overthrew thy reign,
And shattered at a blow the prisoner's chain.

Well was thy doom deserved; thou didst not spare
　　Life's tenderest ties, but cruelly didst part
　　Husband and wife, and from the mother's heart
Didst wrest her children, deaf to shriek and prayer;
　　　　　Thy inner lair became
　　　　　The haunt of guilty shame;
Thy lash dropped blood; the murderer, at thy side,

Showed his red hands, nor feared the vengeance due.
Thou didst sow earth with crimes, and, far and wide,
   A harvest of uncounted miseries grew,
Until the measure of thy sins at last
Was full, and then the avenging bolt was cast!

Go now, accursed of God, and take thy place
   With hateful memories of the elder time,
   With many a wasting plague, and nameless crime,
And bloody war that thinned the human race;
         With the Black Death, whose way
         Through wailing cities lay,
Worship of Moloch, tyrannies that built
   The Pyramids, and cruel creeds that taught
To avenge a fancied guilt by deeper guilt—
   Death at the stake to those that held them not.
Lo! the foul phantoms, silent in the gloom
Of the flown ages, part to yield thee room.

I see the better years that hasten by
   Carry thee back into that shadowy past,
   Where, in the dusty spaces, void and vast,
The graves of those whom thou hast murdered lie.
         The slave-pen, through whose door
         Thy victims pass no more,
Is there, and there shall the grim block remain
   At which the slave was sold; while at thy feet
Scourges and engines of restraint and pain
   Moulder and rust by thine eternal seat.
There, mid the symbols that proclaim thy crimes,
Dwell thou, a warning to the coming times.

May, 1866.

Boston Hymn

Read in Music Hall, January 1, 1863

The word of the Lord by night
To the watching Pilgrims came,
As they sat by the seaside,
And filled their hearts with flame.

God said, I am tired of kings,
I suffer them no more;
Up to my ear the morning brings
The outrage of the poor.

Think ye I made this ball
A field of havoc and war,
Where tyrants great and tyrants small
Might harry the weak and poor?

My angel,—his name is Freedom,—
Choose him to be your king;
He shall cut pathways east and west,
And fend you with his wing.

Lo! I uncover the land
Which I hid of old time in the West,
As the sculptor uncovers the statue
When he has wrought his best;

I show Columbia, of the rocks
Which dip their foot in the seas,
And soar to the air-borne flocks
Of clouds, and the boreal fleece.

I will divide my goods;
Call in the wretch and slave:
None shall rule but the humble,
And none but Toil shall have.

I will have never a noble,
No lineage counted great;
Fishers and choppers and ploughmen
Shall constitute a state.

Go, cut down trees in the forest,
And trim the straightest boughs;
Cut down trees in the forest,
And build me a wooden house.

Call the people together,
The young men and the sires,
The digger in the harvest field,
Hireling, and him that hires;

And here in a pine state-house
They shall choose men to rule
In every needful faculty,
In church, and state, and school

Lo, now! if these poor men
Can govern the land and sea,

And make just laws below the sun,
As planets faithful be.

And ye shall succor men;
'T is nobleness to serve;
Help them who cannot help again:
Beware from right to swerve.

I break your bonds and masterships,
And I unchain the slave:
Free be his heart and hand henceforth
As wind and wandering wave.

I cause from every creature
His proper good to flow:
As much as he is and doeth,
So much he shall bestow.

But, laying hands on another
To coin his labor and sweat,
He goes in pawn to his victim
For eternal years in debt.

To-day unbind the captive,
So only are ye unbound;
Lift up a people from the dust,
Trump of their rescue, sound!

Pay ransom to the owner,
And fill the bag to the brim.
Who is the owner? The slave is owner,
And ever was. Pay him.

O North! give him beauty for rags,
And honor, O South! for his shame;
Nevada! coin thy golden crags
With Freedom's image and name.

Up! and the dusky race
That sat in darkness long,—
Be swift their feet as antelopes,
And as behemoth strong.

Come, East and West and North,
By races, as snow-flakes,
And carry my purpose forth,
Which neither halts nor shakes.

My will fulfilled shall be,
For, in daylight or in dark,
My thunderbolt has eyes to see
His way home to the mark.

Ode—"Do Ye Quail?"

I.

Do ye quail but to hear, Carolinians,
The first foot-tramp of Tyranny's minions?
Have ye buckled on armor, and brandished the spear,
But to shrink with the trumpet's first peal on the ear?
Why your forts now embattled on headland and height,
Your sons all in armor, unless for the fight?
Did ye think the mere show of your guns on the wall,
And your shouts, would the souls of the heathen appal?
That his lusts and his appetites, greedy as Hell,
Led by Mammon and Moloch, would sink at a spell;—
Nor strive, with the tiger's own thirst, lest the flesh
Should be torn from his jaws, while yet bleeding afresh.

II.

For shame! To the breach, Carolinians!—
To the death for your sacred dominions!—
Homes, shrines, and your cities all reeking in flame,
Cry aloud to your souls, in their sorrow and shame;
Your greybeards, with necks in the halter—
Your virgins, defiled at the altar,—
In the loathsome embrace of the felon and slave,
Touch loathsomer far than the worm of the grave!
Ah! God! if you fail in this moment of gloom!

How base were the weakness, how horrid the doom!
With the fiends in your streets howling pæans,
And the Beast o'er another Orleans!

III.

Do ye quail, as on yon little islet
They have planted the feet that defile it?
Make its sands pure of taint, by the stroke of the sword,
And by torrents of blood in red sacrifice pour'd!
Doubts are Traitors, if once they persuade you to fear,
That the foe, in his foothold, is safe from your spear!
When the foot of pollution is set on your shores,
What sinew and soul should be stronger than yours?
By the fame—by the shame—of your sires,
Set on, though each freeman expires;
Better fall, grappling fast with the foe, to their graves,
Than groan in your fetters, the slaves of your slaves.

IV.

The voice of your loud exultation
Hath rung, like a trump, through the nation,
How loudly, how proudly, of deeds to be done,
The blood of the sire in the veins of the son!
Old Moultrie and Sumter still keep at your gates,
And the foe in his foothold as patiently waits.
He asks, with a taunt, by your patience made bold,
If the hot spur of Percy grows suddenly cold—
Makes merry with boasts of your city his own,
And the Chivalry fled, ere his trumpet is blown;
Upon them, O sons of the mighty of yore,
And fatten the sands with their Sodomite gore!

V.

Where's the dastard that cowers and falters
In the sight of his hearthstones and altars?
With the faith of the free in the God of the brave,
Go forth; ye are mighty to conquer and save!
By the blue Heaven shining above ye,
By the pure-hearted thousands that love ye,
Ye are armed with a might to prevail in the fight,
And an ægis to shield and a weapon to smite!
Then fail not, and quail not; the foe shall prevail not:
With the faith and the will, ye shall conquer him still.
To the knife—with the knife, Carolinians,
For your homes, and your sacred dominions.

The Witnesses

In Ocean's wide domains,
    Half buried in the sands,
Lie skeletons in chains,
    With shackled feet and hands.

Beyond the fall of dews,
    Deeper than plummet lies,
Float ships, with all their crews,
    No more to sink nor rise.

There the black Slave-ship swims,
    Freighted with human forms,
Whose fettered, fleshless limbs
    Are not the sport of storms.

There are the bones of Slaves;
    They gleam from the abyss;
They cry, from yawning waves,
    "We are the Witnesses!"

Within Earth's wide domains
    Are markets for men's lives;
Their necks are galled with chains,
    Their wrists are cramped with gyves.

Dead bodies, that the kite
  In deserts makes its prey;
Murders, that with affright
  Scare school-boys from their play!

All evil thoughts and deeds;
  Anger, and lust, and pride;
The foulest, rankest weeds,
  That choke Life's groaning tide!

These are the woes of Slaves;
  They glare from the abyss;
They cry, from unknown graves,
  "We are the Witnesses!"

The Warning

Beware! The Israelite of old, who tore
  The lion in his path,—when, poor and blind,
He saw the blessed light of heaven no more,
  Shorn of his noble strength and forced to grind
In prison, and at last led forth to be
A pander to Philistine revelry,—

Upon the pillars of the temple laid
  His desperate hands, and in its overthrow
Destroyed himself, and with him those who made
  A cruel mockery of his sightless woe;
The poor, blind Slave, the scoff and jest of all,
Expired, and thousands perished in the fall!

There is a poor, blind Samson in this land,
    Shorn of his strength and bound in bonds of steel,
Who may, in some grim revel, raise his hand,
    And shake the pillars of this Commonweal,
Till the vast Temple of our liberties
A shapeless mass of wreck and rubbish lies.

The Cumberland

At anchor in Hampton Roads we lay,
    On board of the Cumberland, sloop-of-war;
And at times from the fortress across the bay
        The alarum of drums swept past,
        Or a bugle blast
    From the camp on the shore.

Then far away to the south uprose
    A little feather of snow-white smoke,
And we knew that the iron ship of our foes
        Was steadily steering its course
        To try the force
    Of our ribs of oak.

Down upon us heavily runs,
    Silent and sullen, the floating fort;
Then comes a puff of smoke from her guns,
        And leaps the terrible death,
        With fiery breath,
    From each open port.

We are not idle, but send her straight
    Defiance back in a full broadside!
As hail rebounds from a roof of slate,
        Rebounds our heavier hail
        From each iron scale
    Of the monster's hide.

"Strike your flag!" the rebel cries,
    In his arrogant old plantation strain.
"Never!" our gallant Morris replies;
        "It is better to sink than to yield!"
        And the whole air pealed
    With the cheers of our men.

Then, like a kraken huge and black,
    She crushed our ribs in her iron grasp!
Down went the Cumberland all a wrack,
        With a sudden shudder of death,
        And the cannon's breath
    For her dying gasp.

Next morn, as the sun rose over the bay,
    Still floated our flag at the mainmast head.
Lord, how beautiful was Thy day!
        Every waft of the air
        Was a whisper of prayer,
    Or a dirge for the dead.

Ho! brave hearts that went down in the seas!
    Ye are at peace in the troubled stream;
Ho! brave land! with hearts like these,
        Thy flag, that is rent in twain,
        Shall be one again,
    And without a seam!

Killed at the Ford

He is dead, the beautiful youth,
The heart of honor, the tongue of truth,
He, the life and light of us all,
Whose voice was blithe as a bugle-call,
Whom all eyes followed with one consent,
The cheer of whose laugh, and whose pleasant word,
Hushed all murmurs of discontent.

Only last night, as we rode along,
Down the dark of the mountain gap,
To visit the picket-guard at the ford,
Little dreaming of any mishap,
He was humming the words of some old song:
"Two red roses he had on his cap
And another he bore at the point of his sword."

Sudden and swift a whistling ball
Came out of a wood, and the voice was still;
Something I heard in the darkness fall,
And for a moment my blood grew chill;
I spake in a whisper, as he who speaks
In a room where some one is lying dead;
But he made no answer to what I said.

We lifted him up to his saddle again,
And through the mire and the mist and the rain
Carried him back to the silent camp,
And laid him as if asleep on his bed;
And I saw by the light of the surgeon's lamp
Two white roses upon his cheeks,
And one, just over his heart, blood-red!

And I saw in a vision how far and fleet
That fatal bullet went speeding forth,
Till it reached a town in the distant North,
Till it reached a house in a sunny street,
Till it reached a heart that ceased to beat
Without a murmur, without a cry;
And a bell was tolled, in that far-off town,
For one who had passed from cross to crown,
And the neighbors wondered that she should die.

A Word for the Hour

The firmament breaks up. In black eclipse
Light after light goes out. One evil star,
Luridly glaring through the smoke of war,
As in the dream of the Apocalypse,
Drags others down. Let us not weakly weep
Nor rashly threaten. Give us grace to keep
Our faith and patience; wherefore should we leap
On one hand into fratricidal fight,
Or, on the other, yield eternal right,
Frame lies of law, and good and ill confound?
What fear we? Safe on freedom's vantage ground
Our feet are planted: let us there remain
In unrevengeful calm, no means untried
Which truth can sanction, no just claim denied,
The sad spectators of a suicide!
They break the links of Union: shall we light
The fires of hell to weld anew the chain
On that red anvil where each blow is pain?
Draw we not even now a freer breath,
As from our shoulders falls a load of death
Loathsome as that the Tuscan's victim bore
When keen with life to a dead horror bound?
Why take we up the accursed thing again?
Pity, forgive, but urge them back no more

Who, drunk with passion, flaunt disunion's rag
With its vile reptile blazon. Let us press
The golden cluster on our brave old flag
In closer union, and, if numbering less,
Brighter shall shine the stars which still remain.

16th, 1st month, 1861.

The Battle Autumn of 1862

The flags of war like storm-birds fly,
   The charging trumpets blow;
Yet rolls no thunder in the sky,
   No earthquake strives below.

And, calm and patient, Nature keeps
   Her ancient promise well,
Though o'er her bloom and greenness sweeps
   The battle's breath of hell.

And still she walks in golden hours
   Through harvest-happy farms,
And still she wears her fruits and flowers
   Like jewels on her arms.

What mean the gladness of the plain,
   This joy of eve and morn,
The mirth that shakes the beard of grain
   And yellow locks of corn?

Ah! eyes may well be full of tears,
   And hearts with hate are hot;

But even-paced come round the years,
　And Nature changes not.

She meets with smiles our bitter grief,
　With songs our groans of pain;
She mocks with tint of flower and leaf
　The war-field's crimson stain.

Still, in the cannon's pause, we hear
　Her sweet thanksgiving-psalm;
Too near to God for doubt or fear,
　She shares th' eternal calm.

She knows the seed lies safe below
　The fires that blast and burn;
For all the tears of blood we sow
　She waits the rich return.

She sees with clearer eye than ours
　The good of suffering born,—
The hearts that blossom like her flowers,
　And ripen like her corn.

O, give to us, in times like these,
　The vision of her eyes;
And make her fields and fruited trees
　Our golden prophecies!

O, give to us her finer ear!
　Above this stormy din,
We too would hear the bells of cheer
　Ring peace and freedom in!

Laus Deo

On hearing the bells ring for the constitutional amendment abolishing slavery in the United States

It is done!
Clang of bell and roar of gun
Send the tidings up and down.
How the belfries rock and reel,
How the great guns, peal on peal,
Fling the joy from town to town!

Ring, O bells!
Every stroke exulting tells
Of the burial hour of crime.
Loud and long, that all may hear,
Ring for every listening ear
Of Eternity and Time!

Let us kneel:
God's own voice is in that peal,
And this spot is holy ground.
Lord, forgive us! What are we,
That our eyes this glory see,
That our ears have heard the sound!

For the Lord
On the whirlwind is abroad;
In the earthquake he has spoken;
He has smitten with his thunder
The iron walls asunder,
And the gates of brass are broken!

Loud and long
 Lift the old exulting song,
Sing with Miriam by the sea:
 He has cast the mighty down;
 Horse and rider sink and drown;
He has triumphed gloriously!

Did we dare,
 In our agony of prayer,
Ask for more than he has done?
 When was ever his right hand
 Over any time or land
Stretched as now beneath the sun!

How they pale,
 Ancient myth, and song, and tale,
In this wonder of our days,
 When the cruel rod of war
 Blossoms white with righteous law,
And the wrath of man is praise.

Blotted out!
 All within and all about
Shall a fresher life begin;
 Freer breathe the universe
 As it rolls its heavy curse
On the dead and buried sin.

It is done!
 In the circuit of the sun
Shall the sound thereof go forth.
 It shall bid the sad rejoice,
 It shall give the dumb a voice,
It shall belt with joy the earth!

Ring and swing
Bells of joy! on morning's wing
Send the song of praise abroad;
With a sound of broken chains,
Tell the nations that He reigns,
Who alone is Lord and God!

Anniversary Poem

(Read before the Alumni of the Friends' Yearly Meeting School, at the Annual Meeting at Newport, R.I., 15th 6th Mo., 1863.)

Once more, dear friends, you meet beneath
    A clouded sky:
Not yet the sword has found its sheath,
And on the sweet spring airs the breath
    Of war floats by.

Yet trouble springs not from the ground,
    Nor pain from chance;
The Eternal order circles round,
And wave and storm find mete and bound
    In Providence.

Full long our feet the flowery ways
    Of peace have trod,
Content with creed and garb and phrase:
A harder path in earlier days
    Led up to God.

Too cheaply truths, once purchased dear,
    Are made our own;
Too long the world has smiled to hear
Our boast of full corn in the ear
    By others sown;

To see us stir the martyr fires
    Of long ago,
And wrap our satisfied desires
In the singed mantles that our sires
    Have dropped below.

But now the cross our worthies bore
    On us is laid;
Profession's quiet sleep is o'er,
And in the scale of truth once more
    Our faith is weighed.

The cry of innocent blood at last
    Is calling down
An answer in the whirlwind-blast,
The thunder and the shadow cast
    From Heaven's dark frown.

The land is red with judgments. Who
    Stands guiltless forth?
Have *we* been faithful as we knew,
To God and to our brother true,
    To Heaven and Earth?

How faint, through din of merchandise
    And count of gain,
Have seemed to us the captive's cries!
How far away the tears and sighs
    Of souls in pain!

This day the fearful reckoning comes
    To each and all;
We hear amidst our peaceful homes
The summons of the conscript drums,
    The bugle's call.

Our path is plain; the war-net draws
    Round us in vain,
While, faithful to the Higher Cause,
We keep our fealty to the laws
    Through patient pain.

The levelled gun, the battle brand,
    We may not take;
But, calmly loyal, we can stand
And suffer with our suffering land
    For conscience' sake.

Why ask for ease where all is pain?
    Shall *we* alone
Be left to add our gain to gain.
When over Armageddon's plain
    The trump is blown?

To suffer well is well to serve;
    Safe in our Lord
The rigid lines of law shall curve
To spare us; from our heads shall swerve
    Its smiting sword.

And light is mingled with the gloom,
    And joy with grief;
Divinest compensations come,
Through thorns of judgment mercies bloom
    In sweet relief.

Thanks for our privilege to bless,
    By word and deed,
The widow in her keen distress,
The childless and the fatherless,
    The hearts that bleed!

For fields of duty, opening wide,
    Where all our powers
Are tasked the eager steps to guide
Of millions on a path untried:
    THE SLAVE IS OURS!

Ours by traditions dear and old,
    Which make the race
Our wards to cherish and uphold,
And cast their freedom in the mould
    Of Christian grace.

And we may tread the sick-bed floors
    Where strong men pine,
And, down the groaning corridors,
Pour freely from our liberal stores
    The oil and wine.

Who murmurs that in these dark days
    His lot is cast?
God's hand within the shadow lays
The stones whereon His gates of praise
    Shall rise at last.

Turn and o'erturn, O outstretched Hand!
    Nor stint, nor stay;
The years have never dropped their sand
On mortal issue vast and grand
    As ours to-day.

Already, on the sable ground
    Of man's despair
Is Freedom's glorious picture found
With all its dusky hands unbound
    Upraised in prayer.

O, small shall seem all sacrifice
    And pain and loss,
When God shall wipe the weeping eyes,
For suffering give the victor's prize,
    The crown for cross!

Barbara Frietchie

Up from the meadows rich with corn,
Clear in the cool September morn,

The clustered spires of Frederick stand
Green-walled by the hills of Maryland.

Round about them orchards sweep,
Apple- and peach-tree fruited deep,

Fair as a garden of the Lord
To the eyes of the famished rebel horde,

On that pleasant morn of the early fall
When Lee marched over the mountain wall,—

Over the mountains winding down,
Horse and foot, into Frederick town.

Forty flags with their silver stars,
Forty flags with their crimson bars,

Flapped in the morning wind: the sun
Of noon looked down, and saw not one.

Up rose old Barbara Frietchie then,
Bowed with her fourscore years and ten;

Bravest of all in Frederick town,
She took up the flag the men hauled down;

In her attic-window the staff she set,
To show that one heart was loyal yet.

Up the street came the rebel tread,
Stonewall Jackson riding ahead.

Under his slouched hat left and right
He glanced: the old flag met his sight.

"Halt!"—the dust-brown ranks stood fast.
"Fire!"—out blazed the rifle-blast.

It shivered the window, pane and sash;
It rent the banner with seam and gash.

Quick, as it fell, from the broken staff
Dame Barbara snatched the silken scarf;

She leaned far out on the window-sill,
And shook it forth with a royal will.

"Shoot, if you must, this old gray head,
But spare your country's flag," she said.

A shade of sadness, a blush of shame,
Over the face of the leader came;

The nobler nature within him stirred
To life at the woman's deed and word:

"Who touches a hair of yon gray head
Dies like a dog! March on!" he said.

All day long through Frederick street
Sounded the tread of marching feet:

All day long that free flag tost
Over the heads of the rebel host.

Ever its torn fields rose and fell
On the loyal winds that loved it well;

And through the hill-gaps sunset light
Shone over it with a warm good-night.

Barbara Frietchie's work is o'er,
And the Rebel rides on his raids no more.

Honor to her! and let a tear
Fall, for her sake, on Stonewall's bier.

Over Barbara Frietchie's grave
Flag of Freedom and Union, wave!

Peace and order and beauty draw
Round thy symbol of light and law;

And ever the stars above look down
On thy stars below in Frederick town!

OLIVER WENDELL HOLMES | 1809–1894

To Canaan

A Puritan War-Song

Where are you going, soldiers,
   With banner, gun, and sword?
We're marching South to Canaan
   To battle for the Lord!
What Captain leads your armies
   Along the rebel coasts?
The Mighty One of Israel,
   His name is Lord of Hosts!
      To Canaan, to Canaan
      The Lord has led us forth,
      To blow before the heathen walls
      The trumpets of the North!

What flag is this you carry
   Along the sea and shore?
The same our grandsires lifted up,—
   The same our fathers bore!
In many a battle's tempest
   It shed the crimson rain,—
What God has woven in his loom
   Let no man rend in twain!
      To Canaan, to Canaan
      The Lord has led us forth,

To plant upon the rebel towers
The banners of the North!

What troop is this that follows,
    All armed with picks and spades?[*]
These are the swarthy bondsmen,—
    The iron-skin brigades!
They'll pile up Freedom's breastwork,
    They'll scoop out rebels' graves;
Who then will be their owner
    And march them off for slaves?
            To Canaan, to Canaan
            The Lord has led us forth,
            To strike upon the captive's chain
            The hammers of the North!

What song is this you're singing?
    The same that Israel sung
When Moses led the mighty choir,
    And Miriam's timbrel rung!
To Canaan! To Canaan!
    The priests and maidens cried:
To Canaan! To Canaan!
    The people's voice replied.
            To Canaan, to Canaan
            The Lord has led us forth,
            To thunder through its adder dens
            The anthems of the North!

[*]The captured slaves were at this time organized as pioneers.

When Canaan's hosts are scattered,
  And all her walls lie flat,
What follows next in order?
  —The Lord will see to that!
We'll break the tyrant's sceptre,—
  We'll build the people's throne,—
When half the world is Freedom's,
  Then all the word's our own!

      To Canaan, to Canaan
      The Lord has led us forth,
      To sweep the rebel threshing-floors,
      A whirlwind from the North!

August 12, 1862.

JULIA WARD HOWE | 1819–1910

Battle-Hymn of the Republic

Mine eyes have seen the glory of the coming of the
    Lord:
He is trampling out the vintage where the grapes of
    wrath are stored;
He hath loosed the fateful lightning of his terrible swift
    sword:
        His truth is marching on.

I have seen Him in the watch-fires of a hundred circling
    camps;
They have builded Him an altar in the evening dews
    and damps;
I can read His righteous sentence by the dim and flaring
    lamps.
        His day is marching on.

I have read a fiery gospel, writ in burnished rows of
    steel:
"As ye deal with my contemners, so with you my grace
    shall deal;
Let the Hero, born of woman, crush the serpent with
    his heel,
        Since God is marching on."

He has sounded forth the trumpet that shall never call
retreat;
He is sifting out the hearts of men before his judgment-
seat:
Oh! be swift, my soul, to answer Him! be jubilant, my
feet!
Our God is marching on.

In the beauty of the lilies Christ was born across the sea,
With a glory in his bosom that transfigures you and me:
As he died to make men holy, let us die to make men
free,
While God is marching on.

JAMES RUSSELL LOWELL | 1819–1891

Ode Recited at the Harvard Commemoration
July 21, 1865

I.

Weak-winged is song,
    Nor aims at that clear-ethered height
Whither the brave deed climbs for light:
    We seem to do them wrong,
Bringing our robin's-leaf to deck their hearse
Who in warm life-blood wrote their nobler verse,
Our trivial song to honor those who come
With ears attuned to strenuous trump and drum,
And shaped in squadron-strophes their desire,
Live battle-odes whose lines were steel and fire:
    Yet sometimes feathered words are strong,
A gracious memory to buoy up and save
From Lethe's dreamless ooze, the common grave
    Of the unventurous throng.

II.

To-day our Reverend Mother welcomes back
  Her wisest Scholars, those who understood
The deeper teaching of her mystic tome,
    And offered their fresh lives to make it good:
        No lore of Greece or Rome,
No science peddling with the names of things,

Or reading stars to find inglorious fates,
            Can lift our life with wings
Far from Death's idle gulf that for the many waits,
            And lengthen out our dates
With that clear fame whose memory sings
In manly hearts to come, and nerves them and dilates:
Nor such thy teaching, Mother of us all!
            Not such the trumpet-call
            Of thy diviner mood,
            That could thy sons entice
From happy homes and toils, the fruitful nest
Of those half-virtues which the world calls best,
            Into War's tumult rude;
            But rather far that stern device
The sponsors chose that round thy cradle stood
            In the dim, unventured wood,
            The VERITAS that lurks beneath
            The letter's unprolific sheath,
    Life of whate'er makes life worth living,
Seed-grain of high emprise, immortal food,
    One heavenly thing whereof earth hath the giving.

III.

Many loved Truth, and lavished life's best oil
    Amid the dust of books to find her,
Content at last, for guerdon of their toil,
    With the cast mantle she hath left behind her.
        Many in sad faith sought for her,
        Many with crossed hands sighed for her;
        But these, our brothers, fought for her,
        At life's dear peril wrought for her,

So loved her that they died for her,
Tasting the raptured fleetness
Of her divine completeness:
    Their higher instinct knew
Those love her best who to themselves are true,
And what they dare to dream of dare to do;
    They followed her and found her
    Where all may hope to find,
Not in the ashes of the burnt-out mind,
But beautiful, with danger's sweetness round her;
    Where faith made whole with deed
    Breathes its awakening breath
    Into the lifeless creed,
    They saw her plumed and mailed,
    With sweet stern face unveiled,
And all-repaying eyes, look proud on them in death.

IV.

Our slender life runs rippling by, and glides
    Into the silent hollow of the past;
        What is there that abides
    To make the next age better for the last?
        Is earth too poor to give us
    Something to live for here that shall outlive us?
        Some more substantial boon
Than such as flows and ebbs with Fortune's fickle moon?
        The little that we see
        From doubt is never free;
        The little that we do
        Is but half-nobly true;
        With our laborious hiving

What men call treasure, and the gods call dross,
    Life seems a jest of Fate's contriving,
    Only secure in every one's conniving,
A long account of nothings paid with loss,
Where we poor puppets, jerked by unseen wires,
    After our little hour of strut and rave,
With all our pasteboard passions and desires,
Loves, hates, ambitions, and immortal fires,
    Are tossed pell-mell together in the grave.
    But stay! no age was e'er degenerate,
    Unless men held it at too cheap a rate,
    For in our likeness still we shape our fate;
        Ah, there is something here
    Unfathomed by the cynic's sneer,
    Something that gives our feeble light
    A high immunity from Night,
    Something that leaps life's narrow bars
    To claim its birthright with the hosts of heaven;
        A seed of sunshine that doth leaven
    Our earthly dulness with the beams of stars,
            And glorify our clay
    With light from fountains elder than the Day;
        A conscience more divine than we,
        A gladness fed with secret tears,
        A vexing, forward-reaching sense
        Of some more noble permanence;
            A light across the sea,
    Which haunts the soul and will not let it be,
Still glimmering from the heights of undegenerate
        years.

V.

Whither leads the path
To ampler fates that leads?
Not down through flowery meads,
To reap an aftermath
Of youth's vainglorious weeds,
But up the steep, amid the wrath
And shock of deadly-hostile creeds,
Where the world's best hope and stay
By battle's flashes gropes a desperate way,
And every turf the fierce foot clings to bleeds.
Peace hath her not ignoble wreath,
Ere yet the sharp, decisive word
Light the black lips of cannon, and the sword
Dreams in its easeful sheath;
But some day the live coal behind the thought,
Whether from Baäl's stone obscene,
Or from the shrine serene
Of God's pure altar brought,
Bursts up in flame; the war of tongue and pen
Learns with what deadly purpose it was fraught,
And, helpless in the fiery passion caught,
Shakes all the pillared state with shock of men:
Some day the soft Ideal that we wooed
Confronts us fiercely, foe-beset, pursued,
And cries reproachful: "Was it, then, my praise,
And not myself was loved? Prove now thy truth;
I claim of thee the promise of thy youth;
Give me thy life, or cower in empty phrase,
The victim of thy genius, not its mate!"
  Life may be given in many ways,

And loyalty to Truth be sealed
As bravely in the closet as the field,
    So bountiful is Fate;
    But then to stand beside her,
    When craven churls deride her,
To front a lie in arms and not to yield,
    This shows, methinks, God's plan
    And measure of a stalwart man,
    Limbed like the old heroic breeds,
    Who stands self-poised on manhood's solid earth,
    Not forced to frame excuses for his birth,
Fed from within with all the strength he needs.

    VI.

Such was he, our Martyr-Chief,
    Whom late the Nation he had led,
    With ashes on her head,
Wept with the passion of an angry grief:
Forgive me, if from present things I turn
To speak what in my heart will beat and burn,
And hang my wreath on his world-honored urn.
    Nature, they say, doth dote,
    And cannot make a man
    Save on some worn-out plan,
    Repeating us by rote:
For him her Old World moulds aside she threw,
    And, choosing sweet clay from the breast
    Of the unexhausted West,
With stuff untainted shaped a hero new,
Wise, steadfast in the strength of God, and true.
    How beautiful to see

Once more a shepherd of mankind indeed,
Who loved his charge, but never loved to lead;
One whose meek flock the people joyed to be,
    Not lured by any cheat of birth,
    But by his clear-grained human worth,
And brave old wisdom of sincerity!
    They knew that outward grace is dust;
    They could not choose but trust
In that sure-footed mind's unfaltering skill,
    And supple-tempered will
That bent like perfect steel to spring again and thrust.
    His was no lonely mountain-peak of mind,
    Thrusting to thin air o'er our cloudy bars,
    A sea-mark now, now lost in vapors blind;
    Broad prairie rather, genial, level-lined,
    Fruitful and friendly for all human kind,
Yet also nigh to Heaven and loved of loftiest stars.
    Nothing of Europe here,
Or, then, of Europe fronting mornward still,
    Ere any names of Serf and Peer
    Could Nature's equal scheme deface;
    Here was a type of the true elder race,
And one of Plutarch's men talked with us face to face.
    I praise him not; it were too late;
And some innative weakness there must be
In him who condescends to victory
Such as the Present gives, and cannot wait,
    Safe in himself as in a fate.
    So always firmly he:
    He knew to bide his time,
    And can his fame abide,

Still patient in his simple faith sublime,
      Till the wise years decide.
    Great captains, with their guns and drums,
     Disturb our judgment for the hour,
      But at last silence comes;
    These all are gone, and, standing like a tower,
   Our children shall behold his fame,
     The kindly-earnest, brave, foreseeing man,
Sagacious, patient, dreading praise, not blame,
   New birth of our new soil, the first American.

VII.

Long as man's hope insatiate can discern
  Or only guess some more inspiring goal
  Outside of Self, enduring as the pole,
Along whose course the flying axles burn
Of spirits bravely-pitched, earth's manlier brood;
  Long as below we cannot find
The meed that stills the inexorable mind;
So long this faith to some ideal Good,
  Under whatever mortal names it masks,
  Freedom, Law, Country, this ethereal mood
That thanks the Fates for their severer tasks,
  Feeling its challenged pulses leap,
  While others skulk in subterfuges cheap,
And, set in Danger's van, has all the boon it asks,
  Shall win man's praise and woman's love,
  Shall be a wisdom that we set above
All other skills and gifts to culture dear,
  A virtue round whose forehead we inwreathe
  Laurels that with a living passion breathe

When other crowns grow, while we twine them, sear.
　What brings us thronging these high rites to pay,
And seal these hours the noblest of our year,
　Save that our brothers found this better way?

VIII.

We sit here in the Promised Land
　That flows with Freedom's honey and milk;
　But 't was they won it, sword in hand,
Making the nettle danger soft for us as silk.
　We welcome back our bravest and our best;—
　Ah me! not all! some come not with the rest,
Who went forth brave and bright as any here!
I strive to mix some gladness with my strain,
　　　But the sad strings complain,
　　　And will not please the ear;
I sweep them for a pæan, but they wane
　　　Again and yet again
Into a dirge, and die away in pain.
In these brave ranks I only see the gaps,
Thinking of dear ones whom the dumb turf wraps,
Dark to the triumph which they died to gain:
　　Fitlier may others greet the living,
　　For me the past is unforgiving;
　　　I with uncovered head
　　　Salute the sacred dead,
Who went, and who return not.—Say not so!
'T is not the grapes of Canaan that repay,
But the high faith that failed not by the way;
Virtue treads paths that end not in the grave;
No ban of endless night exiles the brave;

And to the saner mind
We rather seem the dead that stayed behind.
Blow, trumpets, all your exultations blow!
For never shall their aureoled presence lack:
I see them muster in a gleaming row,
With ever-youthful brows that nobler show;
We find in our dull road their shining track;
In every nobler mood
We feel the orient of their spirit glow,
Part of our life's unalterable good,
Of all our saintlier aspiration;
They come transfigured back,
Secure from change in their high-hearted ways,
Beautiful evermore, and with the rays
Of morn on their white Shields of Expectation!

IX.

But is there hope to save
Even this ethereal essence from the grave?
What ever 'scaped Oblivion's subtle wrong
Save a few clarion names, or golden threads of song?
Before my musing eye
The mighty ones of old sweep by,
Disvoicëd now and insubstantial things,
As noisy once as we; poor ghosts of kings,
Shadows of empire wholly gone to dust,
And many races, nameless long ago,
To darkness driven by that imperious gust
Of ever-rushing Time that here doth blow:
O visionary world, condition strange,
Where naught abiding is but only Change,

Where the deep-bolted stars themselves still shift and
      range!
   Shall we to more continuance make pretence?
Renown builds tombs; a life-estate is Wit;
            And, bit by bit,
The cunning years steal all from us but woe;
   Leaves are we, whose decays no harvest sow.
            But, when we vanish hence,
   Shall they lie forceless in the dark below,
   Save to make green their little length of sods,
   Or deepen pansies for a year or two,
   Who now to us are shining-sweet as gods?
   Was dying all they had the skill to do?
   That were not fruitless: but the Soul resents
   Such short-lived service, as if blind events
   Ruled without her, or earth could so endure;
   She claims a more divine investiture
   Of longer tenure than Fame's airy rents;
   Whate'er she touches doth her nature share;
   Her inspiration haunts the ennobled air,
            Gives eyes to mountains blind,
   Ears to the deaf earth, voices to the wind,
   And her clear trump sings succor everywhere
   By lonely bivouacs to the wakeful mind;
   For soul inherits all that soul could dare:
            Yea, Manhood hath a wider span
   And larger privilege of life than man.
   The single deed, the private sacrifice,
   So radiant now through proudly-hidden tears,
   Is covered up erelong from mortal eyes
   With thoughtless drift of the deciduous years;

But that high privilege that makes all men peers,
That leap of heart whereby a people rise
                Up to a noble anger's height,
And, flamed on by the Fates, not shrink, but grow more
                bright,
        That swift validity in noble veins,
        Of choosing danger and disdaining shame,
                Of being set on flame
        By the pure fire that flies all contact base,
But wraps its chosen with angelic might,
        These are imperishable gains,
    Sure as the sun, medicinal as light,
    These hold great futures in their lusty reins
And certify to earth a new imperial race.

        x.

        Who now shall sneer?
        Who dare again to say we trace
        Our lines to a plebeian race?
            Roundhead and Cavalier!
Dumb are those names erewhile in battle loud;
Dream-footed as the shadow of a cloud,
        They flit across the ear:
That is best blood that hath most iron in 't
To edge resolve with, pouring without stint
            For what makes manhood dear.
        Tell us not of Plantagenets,
Hapsburgs, and Guelfs, whose thin bloods crawl
Down from some victor in a border-brawl!
        How poor their outworn coronets,
Matched with one leaf of that plain civic wreath

Our brave for honor's blazon shall bequeath,
    Through whose desert a rescued Nation sets
Her heel on treason, and the trumpet hears
Shout victory, tingling Europe's sullen ears
    With vain resentments and more vain regrets!

XI.

Not in anger, not in pride,
Pure from passion's mixture rude
Ever to base earth allied,
But with far-heard gratitude,
Still with heart and voice renewed,
To heroes living and dear martyrs dead,
The strain should close that consecrates our brave.
Lift the heart and lift the head!
Lofty be its mood and grave,
Not without a martial ring,
Not without a prouder tread
And a peal of exultation:
Little right has he to sing
Through whose heart in such an hour
Beats no march of conscious power,
Sweeps no tumult of elation!
'T is no Man we celebrate,
By his country's victories great,
A hero half, and half the whim of Fate,
But the pith and marrow of a Nation
Drawing force from all her men,
Highest, humblest, weakest, all,
For her time of need, and then
Pulsing it again through them,

Till the basest can no longer cower,
Feeling his soul spring up divinely tall,
Touched but in passing by her mantle-hem.
Come back, then, noble pride, for 't is her dower!
      How could poet ever tower,
        If his passions, hopes, and fears,
        If his triumphs and his tears,
      Kept not measure with his people?
Boom, cannon, boom to all the winds and waves!
Clash out, glad bells, from every rocking steeple!
Banners, adance with triumph, bend your staves!
      And from every mountain-peak
      Let beacon-fire to answering beacon speak,
      Katahdin tell Monadnock, Whiteface he,
And so leap on in light from sea to sea,
      Till the glad news be sent
      Across a kindling continent,
  Making earth feel more firm and air breathe braver:
"Be proud! for she is saved, and all have helped to save
      her!
      She that lifts up the manhood of the poor,
      She of the open soul and open door,
      With room about her hearth for all mankind!
      The fire is dreadful in her eyes no more;
      From her bold front the helm she doth unbind,
      Sends all her handmaid armies back to spin,
      And bids her navies, that so lately hurled
      Their crashing battle, hold their thunders in,
      Swimming like birds of calm along the unharmful
      shore.
      No challenge sends she to the elder world,

That looked askance and hated; a light scorn
Plays o'er her mouth, as round her mighty knees
She calls her children back, and waits the morn
Of nobler day, enthroned between her subject seas."

XII.

Bow down, dear Land, for thou hast found release!
  Thy God, in these distempered days,
  Hath taught thee the sure wisdom of His ways,
And through thine enemies hath wrought thy peace!
    Bow down in prayer and praise!
No poorest in thy borders but may now
Lift to the juster skies a man's enfranchised brow.
O Beautiful! my Country! ours once more!
Smoothing thy gold of war-dishevelled hair
O'er such sweet brows as never other wore,
          And letting thy set lips,
          Freed from wrath's pale eclipse,
The rosy edges of their smile lay bare,
What words divine of lover or of poet
Could tell our love and make thee know it,
Among the Nations bright beyond compare?
          What were our lives without thee?
          What all our lives to save thee?
          We reck not what we gave thee;
          We will not dare to doubt thee,
But ask whatever else, and we will dare!

The Portent

(*1859*)

Hanging from the beam,
   Slowly swaying (such the law),
Gaunt the shadow on your green,
    Shenandoah!
The cut is on the crown
(Lo, John Brown),
And the stabs shall heal no more.

Hidden in the cap
   Is the anguish none can draw;
So your future veils its face,
    Shenandoah!
But the streaming beard is shown
(Weird John Brown),
The meteor of the war.

The March into Virginia,

Ending in the First Manassas
(*July, 1861*)

Did all the lets and bars appear
   To every just or larger end,
Whence should come the trust and cheer?
   Youth must its ignorant impulse lend—
Age finds place in the rear.
   All wars are boyish, and are fought by boys,
The champions and enthusiasts of the state:
   Turbid ardors and vain joys
      Not barrenly abate—
   Stimulants to the power mature,
      Preparatives of fate.

Who here forecasteth the event?
What heart but spurns at precedent
And warnings of the wise,
Contemned foreclosures of surprise?
The banners play, the bugles call,
The air is blue and prodigal.
   No berrying party, pleasure-wooed,
No picnic party in the May,
Ever went less loth than they
   Into that leafy neighborhood.
In Bacchic glee they file toward Fate,
Moloch's uninitiate;
Expectancy, and glad surmise
Of battle's unknown mysteries.
All they feel is this: 'tis glory,
A rapture sharp, though transitory,

Yet lasting in belaureled story.
So they gayly go to fight,
Chatting left and laughing right.

But some who this blithe mood present,
    As on in lightsome files they fare,
Shall die experienced ere three days are spent—
    Perish, enlightened by the vollied glare;
Or shame survive, and, like to adamant,
    The throe of Second Manassas share.

Shiloh

A Requiem
(*April, 1862*)

Skimming lightly, wheeling still,
    The swallows fly low
Over the field in clouded days,
    The forest-field of Shiloh—
Over the field where April rain
Solaced the parched ones stretched in pain
Through the pause of night
That followed the Sunday fight
    Around the church of Shiloh—
The church so lone, the log-built one,
That echoed to many a parting groan
      And natural prayer
    Of dying foemen mingled there—
Foemen at morn, but friends at eve—
    Fame or country least their care:

(What like a bullet can undeceive!)
    But now they lie low,
While over them the swallows skim,
    And all is hushed at Shiloh.

Malvern Hill

(*July, 1862*)

Ye elms that wave on Malvern Hill
    In prime of morn and May,
Recall ye how McClellan's men
      Here stood at bay?
While deep within yon forest dim
    Our rigid comrades lay—
Some with the cartridge in their mouth,
Others with fixed arms lifted South—
      Invoking so
The cypress glades? Ah wilds of woe!

The spires of Richmond, late beheld
    Through rifts in musket-haze,
Were closed from view in clouds of dust
      On leaf-walled ways,
Where streamed our wagons in caravan;
    And the Seven Nights and Days
Of march and fast, retreat and fight,
Pinched our grimed faces to ghastly plight—
      Does the elm wood
Recall the haggard beards of blood?

The battle-smoked flag, with stars eclipsed,
    We followed (it never fell!)—
In silence husbanded our strength—
        Received their yell;
Till on this slope we patient turned
    With cannon ordered well;
Reverse we proved was not defeat;
But ah, the sod what thousands meet!—
        Does Malvern Wood
Bethink itself, and muse and brood?

We elms of Malvern Hill
        Remember every thing;
But sap the twig will fill:
Wag the world how it will,
        Leaves must be green in Spring.

The Armies of the Wilderness

(1863–4)

I

Like snows the camps on Southern hills
    Lay all the winter long,
Our levies there in patience stood—
    They stood in patience strong.
On fronting slopes gleamed other camps
    Where faith as firmly clung:
Ah, froward kin! so brave amiss—
    The zealots of the Wrong.

In this strife of brothers
    (*God, hear their country call*),
However it be, whatever betide,
    Let not the just one fall.

Through the pointed glass our soldiers saw
    The base-ball bounding sent;
They could have joined them in their sport
    But for the vale's deep rent.
And others turned the reddish soil,
    Like diggers of graves they bent:
The reddish soil and trenching toil
    Begat presentiment.

Did the Fathers feel mistrust?
    Can no final good be wrought?
Over and over, again and again
    Must the fight for the Right be fought?

They lead a Gray-back to the crag:
    "Your earth-works yonder—tell us, man!"
"A prisoner—no deserter, I,
    Nor one of the tell-tale clan."
His rags they mark: "True-blue like you
    Should wear the color—your Country's, man!"
He grinds his teeth: "However that be,
    Yon earth-works have their plan."

Such brave ones, foully snared
    By Belial's wily plea,
Were faithful unto the evil end—
    Feudal fidelity.

"Well, then, your camps—come, tell the names!"
    Freely he leveled his finger then:
"Yonder—see—are our Georgians; on the crest,
    The Carolinians; lower, past the glen,
Virginians—Alabamians—Mississippians—Kentuckians
    (Follow my finger)—Tennesseeans; and the ten
Camps *there*—ask your grave-pits; they'll tell.
    Halloa! I see the picket-hut, the den
Where I last night lay." "Where's Lee?"
    "In the hearts and bayonets of all yon men!"

The tribes swarm up to war
    As in ages long ago,
Ere the palm of promise leaved
    And the lily of Christ did blow.

Their mounted pickets for miles are spied
    Dotting the lowland plain,
The nearer ones in their veteran-rags—
    Loutish they loll in lazy disdain.
But ours in perilous places bide
    With rifles ready and eyes that strain
Deep through the dim suspected wood
    Where the Rapidan rolls amain.

The Indian has passed away,
    But creeping comes another—
Deadlier far. Picket,
    Take heed—take heed of thy brother!

From a wood-hung height, an outpost lone,
    Crowned with a woodman's fort,
The sentinel looks on a land of dole,
      Like Paran, all amort.
Black chimneys, gigantic in moor-like wastes,
    The scowl of the clouded sky retort;
The hearth is a houseless stone again—
    Ah! where shall the people be sought?

    Since the venom such blastment deals,
      The South should have paused, and thrice,
    Ere with heat of her hate she hatched
      The egg with the cockatrice.

A path down the mountain winds to the glade
    Where the dead of the Moonlight Fight lie low;
A hand reaches out of the thin-lain mould
    As begging help which none can bestow.
But the field-mouse small and busy ant
    Heap their hillocks, to hide if they may the woe:
By the bubbling spring lies the rusted canteen,
    And the drum which the drummer-boy dying let go.

    Dust to dust, and blood for blood—
      Passion and pangs! Has Time
    Gone back? or is this the Age
      Of the world's great Prime?

The wagon mired and cannon dragged
    Have trenched their scar; the plain
Tramped like the cindery beach of the damned—
    A site for the city of Cain.

And stumps of forests for dreary leagues
    Like a massacre show. The armies have lain
By fires where gums and balms did burn,
    And the seeds of Summer's reign.

    Where are the birds and boys?
        Who shall go chestnutting when
    October returns? The nuts—
        O, long ere they grow again.

They snug their huts with the chapel-pews,
    In court-houses stable their steeds—
Kindle their fires with indentures and bonds,
    And old Lord Fairfax's parchment deeds;
And Virginian gentlemen's libraries old—
    Books which only the scholar heeds—
Are flung to his kennel. It is ravage and range,
    And gardens are left to weeds.

    Turned adrift into war
        Man runs wild on the plain,
    Like the jennets let loose
        On the Pampas—zebras again.

Like the Pleiads dim, see the tents through the storm—
    Aloft by the hill-side hamlet's graves,
On a head-stone used for a hearth-stone there
    The water is bubbling for punch for our braves.
What if the night be drear, and the blast
    Ghostly shrieks? their rollicking staves

Make frolic the heart; beating time with their swords,
   What care they if Winter raves?

Is life but a dream? and so,
   In the dream do men laugh aloud?
So strange seems mirth in a camp,
   So like a white tent to a shroud.

II

The May-weed springs; and comes a Man
   And mounts our Signal Hill;
A quiet Man, and plain in garb—
   Briefly he looks his fill,
Then drops his gray eye on the ground,
   Like a loaded mortar he is still:
Meekness and grimness meet in him—
   The silent General.

Were men but strong and wise,
   Honest as Grant, and calm,
War would be left to the red and black ants,
   And the happy world disarm.

That eve a stir was in the camps,
   Forerunning quiet soon to come
Among the streets of beechen huts
   No more to know the drum.
The weed shall choke the lowly door,
   And foxes peer within the gloom,
Till scared perchance by Mosby's prowling men,
   Who ride in the rear of doom.

Far West, and farther South,
  Wherever the sword has been,
Deserted camps are met,
  And desert graves are seen.

The livelong night they ford the flood;
  With guns held high they silent press,
Till shimmers the grass in their bayonets' sheen—
  On Morning's banks their ranks they dress;
Then by the forests lightly wind,
  Whose waving boughs the pennons seem to bless,
Borne by the cavalry scouting on—
  Sounding the Wilderness.

Like shoals of fish in spring
  That visit Crusoe's isle,
The host in the lonesome place—
  The hundred thousand file.

The foe that held his guarded hills
  Must speed to woods afar;
For the scheme that was nursed by the Culpepper
      hearth
  With the slowly-smoked cigar—
The scheme that smouldered through winter long
  Now bursts into act—into war—
The resolute scheme of a heart as calm
  As the Cyclone's core.

The fight for the city is fought
  In Nature's old domain;
Man goes out to the wilds,
  And Orpheus' charm is vain.

In glades they meet skull after skull
  Where pine-cones lay—the rusted gun,
Green shoes full of bones, the mouldering coat
  And cuddled-up skeleton;
And scores of such. Some start as in dreams,
  And comrades lost bemoan:
By the edge of those wilds Stonewall had charged—
  But the Year and the Man were gone.

At the height of their madness
  The night winds pause,
Recollecting themselves;
  But no lull in these wars.

A gleam!—a volley! And who shall go
  Storming the swarmers in jungles dread?
No cannon-ball answers, no proxies are sent—
  They rush in the shrapnel's stead.
Plume and sash are vanities now—
  Let them deck the pall of the dead;
They go where the shade is, perhaps into Hades,
  Where the brave of all times have led.

There's a dust of hurrying feet,
  Bitten lips and bated breath,
And drums that challenge to the grave,
  And faces fixed, forefeeling death.

What husky huzzahs in the hazy groves—
    What flying encounters fell;
Pursuer and pursued like ghosts disappear
    In gloomed shade—their end who shall tell?
The crippled, a ragged-barked stick for a crutch,
    Limp to some elfin dell—
Hobble from the sight of dead faces—white
    As pebbles in a well.

    Few burial rites shall be;
        No priest with book and band
    Shall come to the secret place
        Of the corpse in the foeman's land.

Watch and fast, march and fight—clutch your gun!
    Day-fights and night-fights; sore is the stress;
Look, through the pines what line comes on?
    Longstreet slants through the hauntedness!
'Tis charge for charge, and shout for yell:
    Such battles on battles oppress—
But Heaven lent strength, the Right strove well,
    And emerged from the Wilderness.

    Emerged, for the way was won;
        But the Pillar of Smoke that led
    Was brand-like with ghosts that went up
        Ashy and red.

None can narrate that strife in the pines,
    A seal is on it—Sabæan lore!
Obscure as the wood, the entangled rhyme
    But hints at the maze of war—

Vivid glimpses or livid through peopled gloom,
    And fires which creep and char—
A riddle of death, of which the slain
        Sole solvers are.

Long they withhold the roll
    Of the shroudless dead. It is right;
Not yet can we bear the flare
        Of the funeral light.

The College Colonel

He rides at their head;
    A crutch by his saddle just slants in view,
One slung arm is in splints, you see,
    Yet he guides his strong steed—how coldly too.

He brings his regiment home—
    Not as they filed two years before,
But a remnant half-tattered, and battered, and worn,
Like castaway sailors, who—stunned
        By the surf's loud roar,
    Their mates dragged back and seen no more—
Again and again breast the surge,
    And at last crawl, spent, to shore.

A still rigidity and pale—
    An Indian aloofness lones his brow;
He has lived a thousand years

Compressed in battle's pains and prayers,
   Marches and watches slow.

There are welcoming shouts, and flags;
   Old men off hat to the Boy,
Wreaths from gay balconies fall at his feet,
   But to *him*—there comes alloy.

It is not that a leg is lost,
   It is not that an arm is maimed,
It is not that the fever has racked—
   Self he has long disclaimed.

But all through the Seven Days' Fight,
   And deep in the Wilderness grim,
And in the field-hospital tent,
   And Petersburg crater, and dim
Lean brooding in Libby, there came—
   Ah heaven!—what *truth* to him.

Inscription

for Marye's Heights, Fredericksburg

To them who crossed the flood
And climbed the hill, with eyes
   Upon the heavenly flag intent,
   And through the deathful tumult went
Even unto death: to them this Stone—
Erect, where they were overthrown—
   Of more than victory the monument.

A Meditation

ATTRIBUTED TO A NORTHERNER AFTER ATTENDING THE LAST OF TWO FUNERALS FROM THE SAME HOMESTEAD—THOSE OF A NATIONAL AND A CONFEDERATE OFFICER (BROTHERS), HIS KINSMEN, WHO HAD DIED FROM THE EFFECTS OF WOUNDS RECEIVED IN THE CLOSING BATTLES.

How often in the years that close,
   When truce had stilled the sieging gun,
The soldiers, mounting on their works,
   With mutual curious glance have run
From face to face along the fronting show,
And kinsman spied, or friend—even in a foe.

What thoughts conflicting then were shared,
   While sacred tenderness perforce
Welled from the heart and wet the eye;
   And something of a strange remorse
Rebelled against the sanctioned sin of blood,
And Christian wars of natural brotherhood.

Then stirred the god within the breast—
   The witness that is man's at birth;
A deep misgiving undermined
   Each plea and subterfuge of earth;
They felt in that rapt pause, with warning rife,
Horror and anguish for the civil strife.

Of North or South they recked not then,
   Warm passion cursed the cause of war:

Can Africa pay back this blood
    Spilt on Potomac's shore?
Yet doubts, as pangs, were vain the strife to stay,
And hands that fain had clasped again could slay.

How frequent in the camp was seen
    The herald from the hostile one,
A guest and frank companion there
    When the proud formal talk was done;
The pipe of peace was smoked even 'mid the war,
And fields in Mexico again fought o'er.

In Western battle long they lay
    So near opposed in trench or pit,
That foeman unto foeman called
    As men who screened in tavern sit:
"You bravely fight" each to the other said—
"Toss us a biscuit!" o'er the wall it sped.

And pale on those same slopes, a boy—
    A stormer, bled in noon-day glare;
No aid the Blue-coats then could bring,
    He cried to them who nearest were,
And out there came 'mid howling shot and shell
A daring foe who him befriended well.

Mark the great Captains on both sides,
    The soldiers with the broad renown—
They all were messmates on the Hudson's marge,
    Beneath one roof they laid them down;

And, free from hate in many an after pass,
Strove as in school-boy rivalry of the class.

A darker side there is; but doubt
   In Nature's charity hovers there:
If men for new agreement yearn,
   Then old upbraiding best forbear:
"The South's the sinner!" Well, so let it be;
But shall the North sin worse, and stand the Pharisee?

O now that brave men yield the sword,
   Mine be the manful soldier-view;
By how much more they boldly warred,
   By so much more is mercy due:
When Vicksburg fell, and the moody files marched out,
Silent the victors stood, scorning to raise a shout.

WALT WHITMAN | 1819–1892

Cavalry Crossing a Ford

A line in long array where they wind betwixt green
    islands,
They take a serpentine course, their arms flash in the
    sun—hark to the musical clank,
Behold the silvery river, in it the splashing horses
    loitering stop to drink,
Behold the brown-faced men, each group, each person a
    picture, the negligent rest on the saddles,
Some emerge on the opposite bank, others are just
    entering the ford—while,
Scarlet and blue and snowy white,
The guidon flags flutter gayly in the wind.

Bivouac on a Mountain Side

I see before me now a traveling army halting,
Below a fertile valley spread, with barns and the
    orchards of summer,
Behind, the terraced sides of a mountain, abrupt, in
    places rising high,
Broken, with rocks, with clinging cedars, with tall
    shapes dingily seen,

The numerous camp-fires scatter'd near and far, some
　　away up on the mountain,
The shadowy forms of men and horses, looming,
　　large-sized, flickering,
And over all the sky—the sky! far, far out of reach,
　　studded, breaking out, the eternal stars.

The Artilleryman's Vision

While my wife at my side lies slumbering, and the wars
　　are over long,
And my head on the pillow rests at home, and the
　　vacant midnight passes,
And through the stillness, through the dark, I hear, just
　　hear, the breath of my infant,
There in the room as I wake from sleep this vision
　　presses upon me;
The engagement opens there and then in fantasy unreal,
The skirmishers begin, they crawl cautiously ahead, I
　　hear the irregular snap! snap!
I hear the sounds of the different missiles, the short
　　t-h-t! t-h-t! of the rifle-balls,
I see the shells exploding leaving small white clouds, I
　　hear the great shells shrieking as they pass,
The grape like the hum and whirr of wind through the
　　trees, (tumultuous now the contest rages,)
All the scenes at the batteries rise in detail before me
　　again,
The crashing and smoking, the pride of the men in their
　　pieces,

The chief-gunner ranges and sights his piece and selects
    a fuse of the right time,
After firing I see him lean aside and look eagerly off to
    note the effect;
Elsewhere I hear the cry of a regiment charging, (the
    young colonel leads himself this time with
    brandish'd sword,)
I see the gaps cut by the enemy's volleys, (quickly fill'd
    up, no delay,)
I breathe the suffocating smoke, then the flat clouds
    hover low concealing all;
Now a strange lull for a few seconds, not a shot fired on
    either side,
Then resumed the chaos louder than ever, with eager
    calls and orders of officers,
While from some distant part of the field the wind wafts
    to my ears a shout of applause, (some special
    success,)
And ever the sound of the cannon far or near, (rousing
    even in dreams a devilish exultation and all the old
    mad joy in the depths of my soul,)
And ever the hastening of infantry shifting positions,
    batteries, cavalry, moving hither and thither,
(The falling, dying, I heed not, the wounded dripping
    and red I heed not, some to the rear are hobbling,)
Grime, heat, rush, aide-de-camps galloping by or on a
    full run,
With the patter of small arms, the warning *s-s-t* of the
    rifles (these in my vision I hear or see,)
And bombs bursting in air, and at night the vari-color'd
    rockets.

Vigil Strange I Kept on the Field One Night

Vigil strange I kept on the field one night;

When you my son and my comrade dropt at my side
     that day,

One look I but gave which your dear eyes return'd with
     a look I shall never forget,

One touch of your hand to mine O boy, reach'd up as
     you lay on the ground,

Then onward I sped in the battle, the even-contested
     battle,

Till late in the night reliev'd to the place at last again I
     made my way,

Found you in death so cold dear comrade, found your
     body son of responding kisses, (never again on
     earth responding,)

Bared your face in the starlight, curious the scene, cool
     blew the moderate night-wind,

Long there and then in vigil I stood, dimly around me
     the battle-field spreading,

Vigil wondrous and vigil sweet there in the fragrant
     silent night,

But not a tear fell, not even a long-drawn sigh, long,
     long I gazed,

Then on the earth partially reclining sat by your side
     leaning my chin in my hands,

Passing sweet hours, immortal and mystic hours with
     you dearest comrade—not a tear, not a word,

Vigil of silence, love and death, vigil for you my son and
     my soldier,

As onward silently stars aloft, eastward new ones
     upward stole,

Vigil final for you brave boy, (I could not save you, swift
    was your death,
I faithfully loved you and cared for you living, I think
    we shall surely meet again,)
Till at latest lingering of the night, indeed just as the
    dawn appear'd,
My comrade I wrapt in his blanket, envelop'd well his
    form,
Folded the blanket well, tucking it carefully over head
    and carefully under feet,
And there and then and bathed by the rising sun, my
    son in his grave, in his rude-dug grave I deposited,
Ending my vigil strange with that, vigil of night and
    battlefield dim,
Vigil for boy of responding kisses, (never again on earth
    responding,)
Vigil for comrade swiftly slain, vigil I never forget, how
    as day brighten'd,
I rose from the chill ground and folded my soldier well
    in his blanket,
And buried him where he fell.

A March in the Ranks Hard-Prest, and the Road Unknown

A march in the ranks hard-prest, and the road unknown,
A route through a heavy wood with muffled steps in the
    darkness,
Our army foil'd with loss severe, and the sullen remnant
    retreating,

Till after midnight glimmer upon us the lights of a
dim-lighted building,
We come to an open space in the woods, and halt by the
dim-lighted building,
'Tis a large old church at the crossing roads, now an
impromptu hospital,
Entering but for a minute I see a sight beyond all the
pictures and poems ever made,
Shadows of deepest, deepest black, just lit by moving
candles and lamps,
And by one great pitchy torch stationary with wild red
flame and clouds of smoke,
By these, crowds, groups of forms vaguely I see on the
floor, some in the pews laid down,
At my feet more distinctly a solider, a mere lad, in
danger of bleeding to death, (he is shot in the
abdomen,)
I stanch the blood temporarily, (the youngster's face is
white as a lily,)
Then before I depart I sweep my eyes o'er the scene
fain to absorb it all,
Faces, varieties, postures beyond description, most in
obscurity, some of them dead,
Surgeons operating, attendants holding lights, the smell
of ether, the odor of blood,
The crowd, O the crowd of the bloody forms, the yard
outside also fill'd,
Some on the bare ground, some on planks or stretchers,
some in the death-spasm sweating,
An occasional scream or cry, the doctor's shouted orders
or calls,

The glisten of the little steel instruments catching the
    glint of the torches,
These I resume as I chant, I see again the forms, I smell
    the odor,
Then hear outside the orders given, *Fall in, my men,
    fall in;*
But first I bend to the dying lad, his eyes open, a
    half-smile gives he me,
Then the eyes close, calmly close, and I speed forth to
    the darkness,
Resuming, marching, ever in darkness marching, on in
    the ranks,
The unknown road still marching.

The Wound-Dresser

1

An old man bending I come among new faces,
Years looking backward resuming in answer to children,
Come tell us old man, as from young men and maidens
    that love me,
(Arous'd and angry, I'd thought to beat the alarum, and
    urge relentless war,
But soon my fingers fail'd me, my face droop'd and I
    resign'd myself,
To sit by the wounded and soothe them, or silently
    watch the dead;)
Years hence of these scenes, of these furious passions,
    these chances,

Of unsurpass'd heroes, (was one side so brave? the other
was equally brave;)
Now be witness again, paint the mightiest armies of
earth,
Of those armies so rapid so wondrous what saw you to
tell us?
What stays with you latest and deepest? of curious
panics,
Of hard-fought engagements or sieges tremendous what
deepest remains?

2

O maidens and young men I love and that love me,
What you ask of my days those the strangest and sudden
your talking recalls,
Soldier alert I arrive after a long march cover'd with
sweat and dust,
In the nick of time I come, plunge in the fight, loudly
shout in the rush of successful charge,
Enter the captur'd works—yet lo, like a swift-running
river they fade,
Pass and are gone they fade—I dwell not on soldiers'
perils or soldiers' joys,
(Both I remember well—many the hardships, few the
joys, yet I was content.)

But in silence, in dreams' projections,
While the world of gain and appearance and mirth goes
on,
So soon what is over forgotten, and waves wash the
imprints off the sand,

With hinged knees returning I enter the doors, (while
for you up there,
Whoever you are, follow without noise and be of strong
heart.)

Bearing the bandages, water and sponge,
Straight and swift to my wounded I go,
Where they lie on the ground after the battle brought
in,
Where their priceless blood reddens the grass the
ground,
Or to the rows of the hospital tent, or under the roof'd
hospital,
To the long rows of cots up and down each side I return,
To each and all one after another I draw near, not one
do I miss,
An attendant follows holding a tray, he carries a refuse
pail,
Soon to be fill'd with clotted rags and blood, emptied,
and fill'd again.

I onward go, I stop,
With hinged knees and steady hand to dress wounds,
I am firm with each, the pangs are sharp yet
unavoidable,
One turns to me his appealing eyes—poor boy! I never
knew you,
Yet I think I could not refuse this moment to die for
you, if that would save you.

On, on I go, (open doors of time! open hospital doors!)
The crush'd head I dress, (poor crazed hand tear not the
    bandage away,)
The neck of the cavalry-man with the bullet through
    and through I examine,
Hard the breathing rattles, quite glazed already the eye,
    yet life struggles hard,
(Come sweet death! be persuaded O beautiful death!
In mercy come quickly.)

From the stump of the arm, the amputated hand,
I undo the clotted lint, remove the slough, wash off the
    matter and blood,
Back on his pillow the soldier bends with curv'd neck
    and side-falling head,
His eyes are closed, his face is pale, he dares not look on
    the bloody stump,
And has not yet look'd on it.

I dress a wound in the side, deep, deep,
But a day or two more, for see the frame all wasted and
    sinking,
And the yellow-blue countenance see.

I dress the perforated shoulder, the foot with the
    bullet-wound,
Cleanse the one with a gnawing and putrid gangrene, so
    sickening, so offensive,
While the attendant stands behind aside me holding the
    tray and pail.

I am faithful, I do not give out,

The fractur'd thigh, the knee, the wound in the
abdomen,

These and more I dress with impassive hand, (yet deep
in my breast a fire, a burning flame.)

4

Thus in silence in dreams' projections,

Returning, resuming, I thread my way through the
hospitals,

The hurt and wounded I pacify with soothing hand,

I sit by the restless all the dark night, some are so
young,

Some suffer so much, I recall the experience sweet and
sad,

(Many a soldier's loving arms about this neck have
cross'd and rested,

Many a soldier's kiss dwells on these bearded lips.)

Reconciliation

Word over all, beautiful as the sky,

Beautiful that war and all its deeds of carnage must in
time be utterly lost,

That the hands of the sisters Death and Night
incessantly softly wash again, and ever again, this
soil'd world;

For my enemy is dead, a man divine as myself is dead,

I look where he lies white-faced and still in the coffin—I
  draw near,
Bend down and touch lightly with my lips the white face
  in the coffin.

Spirit Whose Work Is Done

(*Washington City, 1865*)

Spirit whose work is done—spirit of dreadful hours!
Ere departing fade from my eyes your forests of
  bayonets;
Spirit of gloomiest fears and doubts, (yet onward ever
  unfaltering pressing,)
Spirit of many a solemn day and many a savage scene—
  electric spirit,
That with muttering voice through the war now closed,
  like a tireless phantom flitted,
Rousing the land with breath of flame, while you beat
  and beat the drum,
Now as the sound of the drum, hollow and harsh to the
  last, reverberates round me,
As your ranks, your immortal ranks, return, return from
  the battles,
As the muskets of the young men yet lean over their
  shoulders,
As I look on the bayonets bristling over their shoulders,
As those slanted bayonets, whole forests of them
  appearing in the distance, approach and pass on,
  returning homeward,

Moving with steady motion, swaying to and fro to the
    right and left,
Evenly lightly rising and falling while the steps keep
    time;
Spirit of hours I knew, all hectic red one day, but pale as
    death next day,
Touch my mouth ere you depart, press my lips close,
Leave me your pulses of rage—bequeath them to me—
    fill me with currents convulsive,
Let them scorch and blister out of my chants when you
    are gone,
Let them identify you to the future in these songs.

O Captain! My Captain!

O Captain! my Captain! our fearful trip is done,
The ship has weather'd every rack, the prize we sought
    is won,
The port is near, the bells I hear, the people all exulting,
While follow eyes the steady keel, the vessel grim and
    daring;
         But O heart! heart! heart!
           O the bleeding drops of red,
             Where on the deck my Captain lies,
             Fallen cold and dead.

O Captain! my Captain! rise up and hear the bells;
Rise up—for you the flag is flung—for you the bugle
    trills,

For you bouquets and ribbon'd wreaths—for you the
     shores a-crowding,
For you they call, the swaying mass, their eager faces
     turning;
          Here Captain! dear father!
               This arm beneath your head!
                    It is some dream that on the deck,
                         You've fallen cold and dead.

My Captain does not answer, his lips are pale and still,
My father does not feel my arm, he has no pulse nor
     will,
The ship is anchor'd safe and sound, its voyage closed
     and done,
From fearful trip the victor ship comes in with object
     won;
          Exult O shores, and ring O bells!
               But I with mournful tread,
                    Walk the deck my Captain lies,
                         Fallen cold and dead.

When Lilacs Last in the Dooryard Bloom'd

1

When lilacs last in the dooryard bloom'd,
And the great star early droop'd in the western sky in
     the night,
I mourn'd, and yet shall mourn with ever-returning
     spring.

Ever-returning spring, trinity sure to me you bring,
Lilac blooming perennial and drooping star in the west,
And thought of him I love.

2

O powerful western fallen star!
O shades of night—O moody, tearful night!
O great star disappear'd—O the black murk that hides
the star!
O cruel hands that hold me powerless—O helpless soul
of me!
O harsh surrounding cloud that will not free my soul.

3

In the dooryard fronting an old farm-house near the
white-wash'd palings,
Stands the lilac-bush tall-growing with heart-shaped
leaves of rich green,
With many a pointed blossom rising delicate, with the
perfume strong I love,
With every leaf a miracle—and from this bush in the
dooryard,
With delicate-color'd blossoms and heart-shaped leaves
of rich green,
A sprig with its flower I break.

4

In the swamp in secluded recesses,
A shy and hidden bird is warbling a song.

Solitary the thrush,
The hermit withdrawn to himself, avoiding the
    settlements,
Sings by himself a song.

Song of the bleeding throat,
Death's outlet song of life, (for well dear brother I know,
If thou was not granted to sing thou would'st surely die.)

5

Over the breast of the spring, the land, amid cities,
Amid lanes and through old woods, where lately the
    violets peep'd from the ground, spotting the gray
    debris,
Amid the grass in the fields each side of the lanes,
    passing the endless grass,
Passing the yellow-spear'd wheat, every grain from its
    shroud in the dark-brown fields uprisen,
Passing the apple-tree blows of white and pink in the
    orchards,
Carrying a corpse to where it shall rest in the grave,
Night and day journeys a coffin.

6

Coffin that passes through lanes and streets,
Through day and night with the great cloud darkening
    the land,
With the pomp of the inloop'd flags with the cities
    draped in black,
With the show of the States themselves as of crape-
    veil'd women standing,

With processions long and winding and the flambeaus
 of the night,
With the countless torches lit, with the silent sea of
 faces and the unbared heads,
With the waiting depot, the arriving coffin, and the
 sombre faces,
With dirges through the night, with the thousand voices
 rising strong and solemn,
With all the mournful voices of the dirges pour'd
 around the coffin,
The dim-lit churches and the shuddering organs—
 where amid these you journey,
With the tolling tolling bells' perpetual clang,
Here, coffin that slowly passes,
I give you my sprig of lilac.

7

(Nor for you, for one alone,
Blossoms and branches green to coffins all I bring,
For fresh as the morning, thus would I chant a song for
 you O sane and sacred death.

All over bouquets of roses,
O death, I cover you over with roses and early lilies,
But mostly and now the lilac that blooms the first,
Copious I break, I break the sprigs from the bushes,
With loaded arms I come, pouring for you,
For you and the coffins all of you O death.)

8

O western orb sailing the heaven,
Now I know what you must have meant as a month
    since I walk'd,
As I walk'd in silence the transparent shadowy night,
As I saw you had something to tell as you bent to me
    night after night,
As you droop'd from the sky low down as if to my side,
    (while the other stars all look'd on,)
As we wander'd together the solemn night, (for
    something I know not what kept me from sleep,)
As the night advanced, and I saw on the rim of the west
    how full you were of woe,
As I stood on the rising ground in the breeze in the cool
    transparent night,
As I watch'd where you pass'd and was lost in the
    netherward black of the night,
As my soul in its trouble dissatisfied sank, as where you
    sad orb,
Concluded, dropt in the night, and was gone.

9

Sing on there in the swamp,
O singer bashful and tender, I hear your notes, I hear
    your call,
I hear, I come presently, I understand you,
But a moment I linger, for the lustrous star has detain'd
    me,
The star my departing comrade holds and detains me.

10

O how shall I warble myself for the dead one there I
    loved?
And how shall I deck my song for the large sweet soul
    that has gone?
And what shall my perfume be for the grave of him I love?

Sea-winds blown from east and west,
Blown from the Eastern sea and blown from the
    Western sea, till there on the prairies meeting,
These and with these and the breath of my chant,
I'll perfume the grave of him I love.

11

O what shall I hang on the chamber walls?
And what shall the pictures be that I hang on the walls,
To adorn the burial-house of him I love?

Pictures of growing spring and farms and homes,
With the Fourth-month eve at sundown, and the gray
    smoke lucid and bright,
With floods of the yellow gold of the gorgeous,
    indolent, sinking sun, burning, expanding the air,
With the fresh sweet herbage under foot, and the pale
    green leaves of the trees prolific,
In the distance the flowing glaze, the breast of the river,
    with a wind-dapple here and there,
With ranging hills on the banks, with many a line
    against the sky, and shadows,
And the city at hand with dwellings so dense, and stacks
    of chimneys,

And all the scenes of life and the workshops, and the
    workmen homeward returning.

12

Lo, body and soul—this land,
My own Manhattan with spires, and the sparkling and
    hurrying tides, and the ships,
The varied and ample land, the South and the North in
    the light, Ohio's shores and flashing Missouri,
And ever the far-spreading prairies cover'd with grass
    and corn.

Lo, the most excellent sun so calm and haughty,
The violet and purple morn with just-felt breezes,
The gentle soft-born measureless light,
The miracle spreading bathing all, the fulfill'd noon,
The coming eve delicious, the welcome night and the
    stars,
Over my cities shining all, enveloping man and land.

13

Sing on, sing on you gray-brown bird,
Sing from the swamps, the recesses, pour your chant
    from the bushes,
Limitless out of the dusk, out of the cedars and pines.

Sing on dearest brother, warble your reedy song,
Loud human song, with voice of uttermost woe.

O liquid and free and tender!
O wild and loose to my soul—O wondrous singer!

You only I hear—yet the star holds me, (but will soon
     depart,)
Yet the lilac with mastering odor holds me.

14

Now while I sat in the day and look'd forth,
In the close of the day with its light and the fields of
     spring, and the farmers preparing their crops,
In the large unconscious scenery of my land with its
     lakes and forests,
In the heavenly aerial beauty, (after the perturb'd winds
     and storms,)
Under the arching heavens of the afternoon swift
     passing, and the voices of children and women,
The many-moving sea-tides, and I saw the ships how
     they sail'd,
And the summer approaching with richness, and the
     fields all busy with labor,
And the infinite separate houses, how they all went on,
     each with its meals and minutia of daily usages,
And the streets how their throbbings throbb'd, and the
     cities pent—lo, then and there,
Falling upon them all and among them all, enveloping
     me with the rest,
Appear'd the cloud, appear'd the long black trail,
And I knew death, its thought, and the sacred
     knowledge of death.

Then with the knowledge of death as walking one side
     of me,

And the thought of death close-walking the other side
    of me,
And I in the middle as with companions, and as holding
    the hands of companions,
I fled forth to the hiding receiving night that talks not,
Down to the shores of the water, the path by the swamp
    in the dimness,
To the solemn shadowy cedars and ghostly pines so still.

And the singer so shy to the rest receiv'd me,
The gray-brown bird I know receiv'd us comrades three,
And he sang the carol of death, and a verse for him I
    love.

From deep secluded recesses,
From the fragrant cedars and the ghostly pines so still,
Came the carol of the bird.

And the charm of the carol rapt me,
As I held as if by their hands my comrades in the night,
And the voice of my spirit tallied the song of the bird.

Come lovely and soothing death,
Undulate round the world, serenely arriving, arriving,
In the day, in the night, to all, to each,
Sooner or later delicate death.

Prais'd be the fathomless universe,
For life and joy, and for objects and knowledge curious,
And for love, sweet love—but praise! praise! praise!
For the sure-enwinding arms of cool-enfolding death.

Dark mother always gliding near with soft feet,
Have none chanted for thee a chant of fullest welcome?
Then I chant it for thee, I glorify thee above all,
I bring thee a song that when thou must indeed come, come
    unfalteringly.

Approach strong deliveress,
When it is so, when thou hast taken them I joyously sing the
    dead,
Lost in the loving floating ocean of thee,
Laved in the flood of thy bliss O death,

From me to thee glad serenades,
Dances for thee I propose saluting thee, adornments and
    feastings for thee,
And the sights of the open landscape and the high-spread sky
    are fitting,
And life and the fields, and the huge and thoughtful night.

The night in silence under many a star,
The ocean shore and the husky whispering wave whose voice I
    know,
And the soul turning to thee O vast and well-veil'd death,
And the body gratefully nestling close to thee.

Over the tree-tops I float thee a song,
Over the rising and sinking waves, over the myriad fields and
    the prairies wide,
Over the dense-pack'd cities all and the teeming wharves and
    ways,
I float this carol with joy, with joy to thee O death.

To the tally of my soul,
Loud and strong kept up the gray-brown bird,
With pure deliberate notes spreading filling the night.

Loud in the pines and cedars dim,
Clear in the freshness moist and the swamp-perfume,
And I with my comrades there in the night.

While my sight that was bound in my eyes unclosed,
As to long panoramas of visions.

And I saw askant the armies,
I saw as in noiseless dreams hundreds of battle-flags,
Borne through the smoke of the battles and pierc'd with
        missiles I saw them,
And carried hither and yon through the smoke, and torn
        and bloody,
And at last but a few shreds left on the staffs, (and all in
        silence,)
And the staffs all splinter'd and broken.

I saw battle-corpses, myriads of them,
And the white skeletons of young men, I saw them,
I saw the debris and debris of all the slain soldiers of the
        war,
But I saw they were not as was thought,
They themselves were fully at rest, they suffer'd not,
The living remain'd and suffer'd, the mother suffer'd,
And the wife and the child and the musing comrade
        suffer'd,
And the armies that remain'd suffer'd.

Passing the visions, passing the night,
Passing, unloosing the hold of my comrades' hands,
Passing the song of the hermit bird and the tallying
    song of my soul,
Victorious song, death's outlet song, yet varying
    ever-altering song,
As low and wailing, yet clear the notes, rising and
    falling, flooding the night,
Sadly sinking and fainting, as warning and warning, and
    yet again bursting with joy,
Covering the earth and filling the spread of the heaven,
As that powerful psalm in the night I heard from
    recesses,
Passing, I leave thee lilac with heart-shaped leaves,
I leave thee there in the door-yard, blooming, returning
    with spring.

I cease from my song for thee,
From my gaze on thee in the west, fronting the west,
    communing with thee,
O comrade lustrous with silver face in the night.

Yet each to keep and all, retrievements out of the night,
The song, the wondrous chant of the gray-brown bird,
And the tallying chant, the echo arous'd in my soul,
With the lustrous and drooping star with the counte-
    nance full of woe,
With the holders holding my hand nearing the call of
    the bird,

Comrades mine and I in the midst, and their memory
     ever to keep, for the dead I loved so well,
For the sweetest, wisest soul of all my days and lands—
     and this for his dear sake,
Lilac and star and bird twined with the chant of my
     soul,
There in the fragrant pines and the cedars dusk and dim.

MARGARET JUNKIN PRESTON | 1820–1897

Hymn to the National Flag

Float aloft, thou stainless banner!
  Azure cross and field of light;
Be thy brilliant stars the symbol
  Of the pure and true and right.
Shelter freedom's holy cause—
Liberty and sacred laws;
Guard the youngest of the nations—
  Keep her virgin honor bright.

From Virginia's storied border,
  Down to Tampa's furthest shore—
From the blue Atlantic's clashings
  To the Rio Grande's roar—
Over many a crimson plain,
Where our martyred ones lie slain—
Fling abroad thy blessed shelter,
  Stream and mount and valley o'er.

In thy cross of heavenly azure
  Has our faith its emblem high;
In thy field of white, the hallow'd
  Truth for which we'll dare and die;
In thy red, the patriot blood—
  Ah! the consecrated flood.

Lift thyself, resistless banner!
  Ever fill our Southern sky!

Flash with living, lightning motion
  In the sight of all the brave!
Tell the price at which we purchased
  Room and right for thee to wave
Freely in our God's free air,
Pure and proud and stainless fair,
Banner of the youngest nation—
  Banner we would die to save!

Strike Thou for us! King of armies!
  Grant us room in Thy broad world!
Loosen all the despot's fetters,
  Back be all his legions hurled!
Give us peace and liberty,
Let the land we love be free—
Then, oh! bright and stainless banner!
  Never shall thy folds be furled!

A Grave in Hollywood Cemetery, Richmond

(*J. R. T.*)

I read the marble-lettered name,
   And half in bitterness I said:
"As Dante from Ravenna came,
   Our poet came from exile—dead."
And yet, had it been asked of him
   Where he would rather lay his head,
This spot he would have chosen. Dim
   The city's hum drifts o'er his grave,
   And green above the hollies wave
Their jagged leaves, as when a boy,
   On blissful summer afternoons,
   He came to sing the birds his runes,
And tell the river of his joy.

Who dreams that in his wanderings wide,
   By stern misfortunes tossed and driven,
   His soul's electric strands were riven
From home and country? Let betide
What might, what would, his boast, his pride,
Was in his stricken mother-land,
   That could but bless and bid him go,
Because no crust was in her hand
   To stay her children's need. We know
The mystic cable sank too deep
   For surface storm or stress to strain,
Or from his answering heart to keep
   The spark from flashing back again!

Think of the thousand mellow rhymes,
    The pure idyllic passion-flowers,
Wherewith, in far gone, happier times,
    He garlanded this South of ours.
Provençal-like, he wandered long,
    And sang at many a stranger's board,
    Yet 't was Virginia's name that poured
The tenderest pathos through his song.
We owe the Poet praise and tears,
    Whose ringing ballad sends the brave,
Bold Stuart riding down the years—
    What have we given him? Just a grave!

HENRY HOWARD BROWNELL | 1820–1872

The Bay Fight
(*Mobile Bay, August 5, 1864*)

"On the forecastle, Ulf the Red
   Watched the lashing of the ships—
'If the Serpent lie so far ahead,
   We shall have hard work of it here,'
      Said he."
                    LONGFELLOW'S *"Saga of King Olaf."*

Three days through sapphire seas we sailed,
   The steady Trade blew strong and free,
The Northern Light his banners paled,
The Ocean Stream our channels wet,
   We rounded low Canaveral's lee,
And passed the isles of emerald set
   In blue Bahama's turquoise sea.

By reef and shoal obscurely mapped,
   And hauntings of the gray sea-wolf,
The palmy Western Key lay lapped
   In the warm washing of the Gulf.

But weary to the hearts of all
   The burning glare, the barren reach
   Of Santa Rosa's withered beach,
And Pensacola's ruined wall.

And weary was the long patrol,
    The thousand miles of shapeless strand,
From Brazos to San Blas that roll
    Their drifting dunes of desert sand.

Yet, coast-wise as we cruised or lay,
    The land-breeze still at nightfall bore,
By beach and fortress-guarded bay,
    Sweet odors from the enemy's shore,

Fresh from the forest solitudes,
    Unchallenged of his sentry lines—
The bursting of his cypress buds,
    And the warm fragrance of his pines.

Ah, never braver bark and crew,
    Nor bolder Flag a foe to dare,
Had left a wake on ocean blue
    Since Lion-Heart sailed *Trenc-le-mer!**

But little gain by that dark ground
    Was ours, save, sometime, freer breath
For friend or brother strangely found,
    'Scaped from the drear domain of death.

And little venture for the bold,
    Or laurel for our valiant Chief,
    Save some blockaded British thief,
Full fraught with murder in his hold,

*The Flag-ship of Richard I.

Caught unawares at ebb or flood—
　Or dull bombardment, day by day,
　With fort and earth-work, far away,
Low couched in sullen leagues of mud.

A weary time,—but to the strong
　The day at last, as ever, came;
And the volcano, laid so long,
　Leaped forth in thunder and in flame!

"Man your starboard battery!"
　Kimberly shouted—
The ship, with her hearts of oak,
Was going, mid roar and smoke,
　　On to victory!
　None of us doubted,
　No, not our dying—
　Farragut's Flag was flying!

Gaines growled low on our left,
　Morgan roared on our right—
Before us, gloomy and fell,
With breath like the fume of hell,
Lay the Dragon of iron shell,
　Driven at last to the fight!

Ha, old ship! do they thrill,
　The brave two hundred scars
　You got in the River-Wars?
That were leeched with clamorous skill,
　(Surgery savage and hard,)

Splinted with bolt and beam,
Probed in scarfing and seam,
   Rudely linted and tarred
With oakum and boiling pitch,
And sutured with splice and hitch,
   At the Brooklyn Navy-Yard!

Our lofty spars were down,
To bide the battle's frown,
(Wont of old renown)—
But every ship was drest
In her bravest and her best,
   As if for a July day;
Sixty flags and three,
   As we floated up the bay—
Every peak and mast-head flew
The brave Red, White, and Blue—
   We were eighteen ships that day.

With hawsers strong and taut,
The weaker lashed to port,
   On we sailed, two by two—
That if either a bolt should feel
Crash through caldron or wheel,
Fin of bronze or sinew of steel,
   Her mate might bear her through.

Steadily nearing the head,
The great Flag-Ship led,
   Grandest of sights!
On her lofty mizen flew

Our Leader's dauntless Blue,
  That had waved o'er twenty fights—
So we went, with the first of the tide,
  Slowly, mid the roar
  Of the Rebel guns ashore
And the thunder of each full broadside.

Ah, how poor the prate
Of statute and state
  We once held with these fellows—
Here, on the flood's pale-green,
  Hark how he bellows,
  Each bluff old Sea-Lawyer!
Talk to them, Dahlgren,
  Parrott, and Sawyer!

On, in the whirling shade
  Of the cannon's sulphury breath,
  We drew to the Line of Death
That our devilish Foe had laid—
Meshed in a horrible net,
  And baited villanous well,
Right in our path were set
  Three hundred traps of hell!

And there, O sight forlorn!
  There, while the cannon
    Hurtled and thundered—
    (Ah, what ill raven
Flapped o'er the ship that morn!)—
Caught by the under-death,

In the drawing of a breath
    Down went dauntless Craven,
      He and his hundred!

A moment we saw her turret,
    A little heel she gave,
And a thin white spray went o'er her,
    Like the crest of a breaking wave—
In that great iron coffin,
    The channel for their grave,
    The fort their monument,
(Seen afar in the offing,)
Ten fathom deep lie Craven,
    And the bravest of our brave.

Then, in that deadly track,
A little the ships held back,
    Closing up in their stations—
There are minutes that fix the fate
    Of battles and of nations,
    (Christening the generations,)
When valor were all too late,
    If a moment's doubt be harbored—
From the main-top, bold and brief,
Came the word of our grand old Chief—
    "Go on!" 'twas all he said—
Our helm was put to starboard,
    And the Hartford passed ahead.

Ahead lay the Tennessee,
    On our starboard bow he lay,

With his mail-clad consorts three,
    (The rest had run up the Bay)—
There he was, belching flame from his bow,
And the steam from his throat's abyss
Was a Dragon's maddened hiss—
    In sooth a most cursèd craft!—
In a sullen ring at bay
By the Middle Ground they lay,
    Raking us fore and aft.

Trust me, our berth was hot,
    Ah, wickedly well they shot;
How their death-bolts howled and stung!
    And the water-batteries played
    With their deadly cannonade
Till the air around us rung;
So the battle raged and roared—
Ah, had you been aboard
    To have seen the fight we made!

How they leaped, the tongues of flame,
    From the cannon's fiery lip!
How the broadsides, deck and frame,
    Shook the great ship!

And how the enemy's shell
    Came crashing, heavy and oft,
    Clouds of splinters flying aloft
And falling in oaken showers—
    But ah, the pluck of the crew!
Had you stood on that deck of ours,
    You had seen what men may do.

Still, as the fray grew louder,
  Boldly they worked and well;
Steadily came the powder,
  Steadily came the shell.
And if tackle or truck found hurt,
  Quickly they cleared the wreck;
And the dead were laid to port,
  All a-row, on our deck.

Never a nerve that failed,
  Never a cheek that paled,
Not a tinge of gloom or pallor—
  There was bold Kentucky's grit,
And the old Virginian valor,
  And the daring Yankee wit.

There were blue eyes from turfy Shannon,
  There were black orbs from palmy Niger—
But there, alongside the cannon,
  Each man fought like a tiger!

A little, once, it looked ill,
  Our consort began to burn—
They quenched the flames with a will,
But our men were falling still,
  And still the fleet was astern.

Right abreast of the Fort
  In an awful shroud they lay,
  Broadsides thundering away,
And lightning from every port—
  Scene of glory and dread!

A storm-cloud all aglow
    With flashes of fiery red—
The thunder raging below,
    And the forest of flags o'erhead!

So grand the hurly and roar,
    So fiercely their broadsides blazed,
The regiments fighting ashore
    Forgot to fire as they gazed.

    There, to silence the Foe,
    Moving grimly and slow,
They loomed in that deadly wreath,
    Where the darkest batteries frowned—
    Death in the air all round,
And the black torpedoes beneath!

And now, as we looked ahead,
    All for'ard, the long white deck
Was growing a strange dull red;
        But soon, as once and agen
Fore and aft we sped,
    (The firing to guide or check,)
You could hardly choose but tread
    On the ghastly human wreck,
(Dreadful gobbet and shred
        That a minute ago were men!)

Red, from main-mast to bitts!
    Red, on bulwark and wale—
Red, by combing and hatch—
    Red, o'er netting and rail!

And ever, with steady con,
  The ship forged slowly by—
And ever the crew fought on,
  And their cheers rang loud and high.

Grand was the sight to see
    How by their guns they stood,
Right in front of our dead
  Fighting square abreast—
  Each brawny arm and chest
All spotted with black and red,
    Chrism of fire and blood!

Worth our watch, dull and sterile,
  Worth all the weary time—
Worth the woe and the peril,
  To stand in that strait sublime!

Fear? A forgotten form!
  Death? A dream of the eyes!
We were atoms in God's great storm
  That roared through the angry skies.

One only doubt was ours,
  One only dread we knew—
Could the day that dawned so well
Go down for the Darker Powers?
  Would the fleet get through?
And ever the shot and shell
Came with the howl of hell,

The splinter-clouds rose and fell,
    And the long line of corpses grew—
    Would the fleet win through?

They are men that never will fail,
    (How aforetime they've fought!)
But Murder may yet prevail—
        They may sink as Craven sank.
    Therewith one hard, fierce thought,
Burning on heart and lip,
Ran like fire through the ship—
        Fight her, to the last plank!

A dimmer Renown might strike
    If Death lay square alongside—
But the Old Flag has no like,
    She must fight, whatever betide—
When the War is a tale of old,
And this day's story is told,
    They shall hear how the Hartford died!

But as we ranged ahead,
    And the leading ships worked in,
    Losing their hope to win
The enemy turned and fled—
And one seeks a shallow reach,
    And another, winged in her flight,
    Our mate, brave Jouett, brings in—
    And one, all torn in the fight,
Runs for a wreck on the beach,
    Where her flames soon fire the night.

And the Ram, when well up the Bay,
    And we looked that our stems should meet,
(He had us fair for a prey,)
Shifting his helm midway,
    Sheered off and ran for the fleet;
There, without skulking or sham,
    He fought them, gun for gun,
And ever he sought to ram,
    But could finish never a one.

From the first of the iron shower
    Till we sent our parting shell,
'Twas just one savage hour
    Of the roar and the rage of hell.

With the lessening smoke and thunder,
    Our glasses around we aim—
What is that burning yonder?
    Our Philippi,—aground and in flame!

Below, 'twas still all a-roar,
As the ships went by the shore,
    But the fire of the Fort had slacked,
(So fierce their volleys had been)—
And now, with a mighty din,
The whole fleet came grandly in,
    Though sorely battered and wracked.

So, up the Bay we ran,
    The Flag to port and ahead;
And a pitying rain began
    To wash the lips of our dead.

A league from the Fort we lay,
    And deemed that the end must lag;
When lo! looking down the Bay,
    There flaunted the Rebel Rag—
The Ram is again underway
    And heading dead for the Flag!

    Steering up with the stream,
        Boldly his course he lay,
Though the fleet all answered his fire,
And, as he still drew nigher,
    Ever on bow and beam
        Our Monitors pounded away—
        How the Chicasaw hammered away!

Quickly breasting the wave,
    Eager the prize to win,
First of us all the brave
    Monongahela went in
Under full head of steam—
Twice she struck him abeam,
Till her stem was a sorry work,
    (She might have run on a crag!)
The Lackawana hit fair,
He flung her aside like cork,
    And still he held for the Flag.

High in the mizen shroud,
    (Lest the smoke his sight o'erwhelm,)
Our Admiral's voice rang loud,
    "Hard-a-starboard your helm!

Starboard! and run him down!"
     Starboard it was—and so,
Like a black squall's lifting frown,
Our mighty bow bore down
     On the iron beak of the Foe.

We stood on the deck together,
     Men that had looked on death
In battle and stormy weather—
     Yet a little we held our breath,
     When, with the hush of death,
The great ships drew together.

Our Captain strode to the bow,
     Drayton, courtly and wise,
     Kindly cynic, and wise,
(You hardly had known him now,
     The flame of fight in his eyes!)
His brave heart eager to feel
How the oak would tell on the steel!

     But, as the space grew short,
          A little he seemed to shun us,
Out peered a form grim and lanky,
     And a voice yelled—"Hard-a-port!
Hard-a-port!—here's the damned Yankee
          Coming right down on us!"

He sheered, but the ships ran foul
With a gnarring shudder and growl—
     He gave us a deadly gun;

But as he passed in his pride,
(Rasping right alongside!)
    The Old Flag, in thunder tones,
Poured in her port broadside,
Rattling his iron hide,
    And cracking his timber bones!

Just then, at speed on the Foe,
    With her bow all weathered and brown,
    The great Lackawana came down,
Full tilt, for another blow;
We were forging ahead,
    She reversed—but, for all our pains,
Rammed the old Hartford, instead,
    Just for'ard the mizzen chains!

Ah! how the masts did buckle and bend,
    And the stout hull ring and reel,
As she took us right on end!
    (Vain were engine and wheel,
    She was under full steam)—
With the roar of a thunder-stroke
Her two thousand tons of oak
    Brought up on us, right abeam!

A wreck, as it looked, we lay—
(Rib and plankshear gave way
    To the stroke of that giant wedge!)
Here, after all, we go—
The old ship is gone!—ah, no,
    But cut to the water's edge.

Never mind, then—at him again!
  His flurry now can't last long;
He'll never again see land—
Try that on *him*, Marchand!
  On him again, brave Strong!

Heading square at the hulk,
  Full on his beam we bore;
But the spine of the huge Sea-Hog
Lay on the tide like a log,
  He vomited flame no more.

By this, he had found it hot—
  Half the fleet, in an angry ring,
  Closed round the hideous Thing,
Hammering with solid shot,
And bearing down, bow on bow—
  He has but a minute to choose;
Life or renown?—which now
  Will the Rebel Admiral lose?

Cruel, haughty, and cold,
He ever was strong and bold—
  Shall he shrink from a wooden stem?
He will think of that brave band
He sank in the Cumberland—
  Aye, he will sink like them.

Nothing left but to fight
Boldly his last sea-fight!
  Can he strike? By heaven, 'tis true!

Down comes the traitor Blue,
And up goes the captive White!

Up went the White! Ah then
The hurrahs that, once and agen,
Rang from three thousand men
    All flushed and savage with fight!
Our dead lay cold and stark,
But our dying, down in the dark,
    Answered as best they might—
Lifting their poor lost arms,
    And cheering for God and Right!

Ended the mighty noise,
    Thunder of forts and ships.
        Down we went to the hold—
O, our dear dying boys!
How we pressed their poor brave lips,
    (Ah, so pallid and cold!)
And held their hands to the last,
    (Those that had hands to hold).

Still thee, O woman heart!
    (So strong an hour ago)—
If the idle tears must start,
    'Tis not in vain they flow.

They died, our children dear,
    On the drear berth deck they died;
Do not think of them here—
Even now their footsteps near

The immortal, tender sphere—
(Land of love and cheer!
 Home of the Crucified!)

And the glorious deed survives.
 Our threescore, quiet and cold,
Lie thus, for a myriad lives
 And treasure-millions untold—
(Labor of poor men's lives,
Hunger of weans and wives,
 Such is war-wasted gold.)

Our ship and her fame to-day
 Shall float on the storied Stream,
When mast and shroud have crumbled away
 And her long white deck is a dream.

One daring leap in the dark,
 Three mortal hours, at the most—
And hell lie stiff and stark
 On a hundred leagues of coast.

For the mighty Gulf is ours—
 The Bay is lost and won,
 An Empire is lost and won!
Land, if thou yet hast flowers,
Twine them in one more wreath
 Of tenderest white and red,
(Twin buds of glory and death!)
 For the brows of our brave dead—
 For thy Navy's noblest Son.

Joy, O Land, for thy sons,
     Victors by flood and field!
The traitor walls and guns
     Have nothing left but to yield—
     (Even now they surrender!)

And the ships shall sail once more,
     And the cloud of war sweep on
To break on the cruel shore—
     But Craven is gone,
     He and his hundred are gone.

The flags flutter up and down
     At sunrise and twilight dim,
The cannons menace and frown—
     But never again for him,
     Him and the hundred.

The Dahlgrens are dumb,
     Dumb are the mortars—
Never more shall the drum
     Beat to colors and quarters—
     The great guns are silent.

O brave heart and loyal!
     Let all your colors dip—
     Mourn him, proud Ship!
From main deck to royal.
     God rest our Captain,
     Rest our lost hundred.

Droop, flag and pennant!
　What is your pride for?
　Heaven, that he died for,
Rest our Lieutenant,
　Rest our brave threescore.

O Mother Land! this weary life
　We led, we lead, is 'long of thee;
Thine the strong agony of strife,
　And thine the lonely sea.

Thine the long decks all slaughter-sprent,
　The weary rows of cots that lie
With wrecks of strong men, marred and rent,
　'Neath Pensacola's sky.

And thine the iron caves and dens
　Wherein the flame our war-fleet drives;
The fiery vaults, whose breath is men's
　Most dear and precious lives.

Ah, ever, when with storm sublime
　Dread Nature clears our murky air,
Thus in the crash of falling crime
　Some lesser guilt must share.

Full red the furnace fires must glow
　That melt the ore of mortal kind:
The Mills of God are grinding slow,
　But ah, how close they grind!

To-day the Dahlgren and the drum
   Are dread Apostles of his Name;
His Kingdom here can only come
   By chrism of blood and flame.

Be strong: already slants the gold
   Athwart these wild and stormy skies;
From out this blackened waste, behold,
   What happy homes shall rise!

But see thou well no traitor gloze,
   No striking hands with Death and Shame,
Betray the sacred blood that flows
   So freely for thy name.

And never fear a victor foe—
   Thy children's hearts are strong and high;
Nor mourn too fondly—well they know
   On deck or field to die.

Nor shalt thou want one willing breath,
   Though, ever smiling round the brave,
The blue sea bear us on to death,
   The green were one wide grave.

U.S. Flag Ship Hartford, Mobile Bay,
   August, 1864.

THOMAS BUCHANAN READ | 1822–1872

Sheridan's Ride

Up from the South at break of day,
Bringing to Winchester fresh dismay,
   The affrighted air with a shudder bore,
   Like a herald in haste, to the chieftain's door,
   The terrible grumble, and rumble, and roar,
   Telling the battle was on once more,
And Sheridan twenty miles away.

And wider still those billows of war,
Thundered along the horizon's bar;
And louder yet into Winchester rolled
The roar of that red sea uncontrolled,
Making the blood of the listener cold,
As he thought of the stake in that fiery fray,
And Sheridan twenty miles away.

But there is a road from Winchester town,
A good broad highway leading down;
And there, through the flush of the morning light,
A steed as black as the steeds of night,
Was seen to pass, as with eagle flight,
As if he knew the terrible need;
He stretched away with his utmost speed;
Hills rose and fell; but his heart was gay,
With Sheridan fifteen miles away.

Still sprung from those swift hoofs, thundering South,
The dust, like smoke from the cannon's mouth;
Or the trail of a comet, sweeping faster and faster,
Foreboding to traitors the doom of disaster.
The heart of the steed, and the heart of the master
Were beating like prisoners assaulting their walls,
Impatient to be where the battle-field calls;
Every nerve of the charger was strained to full play,
With Sheridan only ten miles away.

Under his spurning feet the road
Like an arrowy Alpine river flowed,
And the landscape sped away behind
Like an ocean flying before the wind,
And the steed, like a bark fed with furnace ire,
Swept on, with his wild eye full of fire.
But lo! he is nearing his heart's desire;
He is snuffing the smoke of the roaring fray,
With Sheridan only five miles away.

The first that the general saw were the groups
Of stragglers, and then the retreating troops,
What was done? what to do? a glance told him both,
Then striking his spurs, with a terrible oath,
He dashed down the line, 'mid a storm of huzzas,
And the wave of retreat checked its course there,
        because
The sight of the master compelled it to pause.
With foam and with dust, the black charger was gray;
By the flash of his eye, and the red nostril's play,
He seemed to the whole great army to say,

"I have brought you Sheridan all the way
From Winchester, down to save the day!"

Hurrah! hurrah for Sheridan!
Hurrah! hurrah for horse and man!
And when their statues are placed on high,
Under the dome of the Union sky,
The American soldiers' Temple of Fame;
There with the glorious general's name,
Be it said, in letters both bold and bright,
    "Here is the steed that saved the day,
By carrying Sheridan into the fight,
    From Winchester, twenty miles away!"

The Virginians of the Valley

To William Norborne Nelson

The knightliest of the knightly race
    That, since the days of old,
Have kept the lamp of chivalry
    Alight in hearts of gold;
The kindliest of the kindly band
    That, rarely hating ease,
Yet rode with Spotswood round the land,
    And Raleigh round the seas.

Who climbed the blue Virginia hills
    Against embattled foes,
And planted there, in valleys fair,
    The lily and the rose;
Whose fragrance lives in many lands,
    Whose beauty stars the earth,
And lights the hearths of happy homes
    With loveliness and worth.

We thought they slept!—the sons who kept
    The names of noble sires,
And slumbered while the darkness crept
    Around their vigil fires;

But, aye, the "Golden Horseshoe" Knights
   Their old Dominion keep,
Whose foes have found enchanted ground,
   But not a knight asleep!

Little Giffen

Out of the focal and foremost fire,
Out of the hospital walls as dire,
Smitten of grape-shot and gangrene,
(Eighteenth battle, and he sixteen!)
Specter! such as you seldom see,
Little Giffen, of Tennessee!

"Take him and welcome!" the surgeons said:
Little the doctor can help the dead!
So we took him, and brought him where
The balm was sweet in the summer air;
And we laid him down on a wholesome bed—
Utter Lazarus, heel to head!

And we watched the war with abated breath,
Skeleton boy against skeleton death.
Months of torture, how many such?
Weary weeks of the stick and crutch;
And still a glint of the steel-blue eye
Told of a spirit that wouldn't die.

And didn't. Nay, more! in death's despite
The crippled skeleton learned to write.
"Dear Mother," at first, of course; and then
"Dear Captain," inquiring about the men.
Captain's answer: "Of eighty and five,
Giffen and I are left alive."

Word of gloom from the war, one day;
Johnston pressed at the front, they say.
Little Giffen was up and away;
A tear—his first—as he bade good-by,
Dimmed the glint of his steel-blue eye.
"I'll write, if spared!" There was news of the fight;
But none of Giffen. He did not write.

I sometime fancy that were I king
Of the princely knights of the Golden Ring,
With the song of the minstrel in mine ear,
And the tender legend that trembles here,
I'd give the best on his bended knee,
The whitest soul of my chivalry,
For "Little Giffen," of Tennessee.

Blood, blood! The lines of every printed sheet
    Through their dark arteries reek with running gore;
    At hearth, at board, before the household door,
    'T is the sole subject with which neighbors meet.
Girls at the feast, and children in the street,
    Prattle of horrors; flash their little store
    Of simple jests against the cannon's roar,
    As if mere slaughter kept existence sweet.
O, heaven, I quail at the familiar way
    This fool, the world, disports his jingling cap;
    Murdering or dying with one grin agap!
Our very Love comes draggled from the fray,
    Smiling at victory, scowling at mishap,
    With gory Death companioned and at play.

———

Oh! craven, craven! while my brothers fall,
    Like grass before the mower, in the fight,
    I, easy vassal to my own delight,
    Am bound with flowers, a far too willing thrall.
Day after day along the streets I crawl,
    Shamed in my manhood, reddening at the sight
    Of every soldier who upholds the right
    With no more motive than his country's call.

I love thee more than honor; ay, above
   That simple duty, conscience-plain and clear
   To dullest minds, whose summons all men hear.
Yet as I blush and loiter, who should move
   In the grand marches, I cannot but fear
   That thou wilt scorn me for my very love.

Dirge for a Soldier

In Memory of General Philip Kearny
Killed September 1, 1862.

Close his eyes; his work is done!
   What to him is friend or foeman,
Rise of moon, or set of sun,
   Hand of man, or kiss of woman?
      Lay him low, lay him low,
      In the clover or the snow!
      What cares he? he cannot know:
         Lay him low!

As man may, he fought his fight,
   Proved his truth by his endeavor;
Let him sleep in solemn night,
   Sleep forever and forever,
      Lay him low, lay him low,
      In the clover or the snow!
      What cares he? he cannot know:
         Lay him low!

Fold him in his courtry's stars,
　　Roll the drum and fire the volley!
What to him are all our wars,
　　What but death bemocking folly?
　　　　Lay him low, lay him low,
　　　　In the clover or the snow!
　　　　What cares he? he cannot know:
　　　　　　Lay him low!

Leave him to God's watching eye,
　　Trust him to the hand that made him.
Mortal love weeps idly by:
　　God alone has power to aid him.
　　　　Lay him low, lay him low,
　　　　In the clover or the snow!
　　　　What cares he? he cannot know:
　　　　　　Lay him low!

The Slave Auction

The sale began—young girls were there,
   Defenceless in their wretchedness,
Whose stifled sobs of deep despair
   Revealed their anguish and distress.

And mothers stood, with streaming eyes,
   And saw their dearest children sold;
Unheeded rose their bitter cries,
   While tyrants barter'd them for gold.

And woman, with her love and truth—
   For these in sable forms may dwell—
Gaz'd on the husband of her youth,
   With anguish none may paint or tell.

And men, whose sole crime was their hue,
   The impress of their Maker's hand,
And frail and shrinking children too,
   Were gathered in that mournful band.

Ye who have laid your lov'd to rest,
   And wept above their lifeless clay,
Know not the anguish of that breast,
   Whose lov'd are rudely torn away.

Ye may not know how desolate
　　Are bosoms rudely forced to part,
And how a dull and heavy weight
　　Will press the life-drops from the heart.

FROM **Campaigning**

I heard the bullet's hiss,
  Incessant, sharp and fell,
The keenest, deadliest note
That bursts from battle's throat;
  The piercing screech and jarring whirr
  Of grape and canister;
And flying from afar, the shell
With changeful, throbbing, husky yell,
  A demon tiger, leaping miles
To spread his iron claws
  And tear the bleeding files;
While oft arose the charging cry
  Of men who battled for a glorious cause
And died when it was beautiful to die.

The Storming Column

Do you remember the storming column
  That Banks sent up one night of June?
Do you recall the grandly solemn
  Advance withouten star or moon?
The tangled wood and the boding cry
Of owls that jeered us on to die?

Afar in stifling night we heard
   The picket rattle rise and fall;
Now and then the leaves were stirred
   Above our heads by a random ball;
There were no clamored orders then,
The orders came from whispering men.

Our road by dark battalions ran,
   By sections harnessed, man and steed;
We heard them croak, "There goes the van";
   And then we knew that we should lead
The battle; but our hearts would roam,
And many thought, "Adieu to home."

The colonel groped before the files
   Of bayonets bare and sabres drawn;
We roamed and stumbled dusky miles,
   And night had paled to filmy dawn
When yellow earthworks loomed ahead
And howling battle called our dead.

Then officer and soldier yelled,
   And wildly charged the old brigade;
The hoarse hurrahs one moment quelled
   The rifle crash and cannonade;
I think the very caves of death
Reëchoed that heroic breath.

For the dying shouted as they died,
   Cheering their panting comrades on;
And though the clanging bronze replied,
   They heard it not, for they were gone;

And thus I think their final call
Entered the gates of Odin's hall.

We reached the trench; our foremost dead
    Dotted the smoking mounds with blue;
The bastions flushed with clotting red,
    And still the hissing bullets flew;
They hailed along the gullied banks
And thinned the wearied, broken ranks.

In vain supporting cannon roared,
    In vain renewed battalions pressed;
The Southern flag triumphant soared,
    We could not smoor the flaming crest;
We could not conquer—could but die.
Yet all the war was a victory.

All Quiet Along the Potomac

"All quiet along the Potomac," they say,
 "Except, now and then, a stray picket
Is shot, as he walks on his beat to and fro,
 By a rifleman hid in the thicket.
'Tis nothing—a private or two now and then
 Will not count in the news of the battle;
Not an officer lost—only one of the men
 Moaning out, all alone, the death-rattle."

   *   *   *   *   *

All quiet along the Potomac to-night,
 Where the soldiers lie peacefully dreaming;
Their tents, in the rays of the clear autumn moon
 Or the light of the watch-fire, are gleaming.
A tremulous sigh of the gentle night-wind
 Through the forest-leaves softly is creeping,
While stars up above, with their glittering eyes,
 Keep guard, for the army is sleeping.

There's only the sound of the lone sentry's tread
 As he tramps from the rock to the fountain,
And thinks of the two in the low trundle-bed
 Far away in the cot on the mountain.
His musket falls slack; his face, dark and grim,
 Grows gentle with memories tender

As he mutters a prayer for the children asleep—
	For their mother; may Heaven defend her!

The moon seems to shine just as brightly as then,
	That night when the love yet unspoken
Leaped up to his lips—when low-murmured vows
	Were pledged to be ever unbroken.
Then drawing his sleeve roughly over his eyes,
	He dashes off tears that are welling,
And gathers his gun closer up to its place,
	As if to keep down the heart-swelling.

He passes the fountain, the blasted pine tree,
	The footstep is lagging and weary;
Yet onward he goes through the broad belt of light,
	Toward the shade of the forest so dreary.
Hark! was it the night-wind that rustled the leaves?
	Was it moonlight so wondrously flashing?
It looked like a rifle—"Ha! Mary, good-bye!"
	The red life-blood is ebbing and plashing.

All quiet along the Potomac to-night,
	No sound save the rush of the river;
While soft falls the dew on the face of the dead—
	The picket's off duty for ever!

The Blue and the Gray

"The women of Columbus, Mississippi, animated by nobler sentiments than are many of their sisters, have shown themselves impartial in their offerings made to the memory of the dead. They strewed flowers alike on the graves of the Confederate and of the National soldiers."—NEW YORK TRIBUNE.

By the flow of the inland river,
   Whence the fleets of iron have fled,
Where the blades of the grave-grass quiver,
   Asleep are the ranks of the dead;—
      Under the sod and the dew,
         Waiting the judgment day;—
      Under the one, the Blue;
         Under the other, the Gray.

These in the robings of glory,
   Those in the gloom of defeat,
All with the battle-blood gory,
   In the dusk of eternity meet;—
      Under the sod and the dew,
         Waiting the judgment day;—
      Under the laurel, the Blue;
         Under the willow, the Gray.

From the silence of sorrowful hours
   The desolate mourners go,
Lovingly laden with flowers
   Alike for the friend and the foe;—

Under the sod and the dew,
    Waiting the judgment day;—
Under the roses, the Blue;
    Under the lilies, the Gray.

So with an equal splendor
    The morning sun-rays fall,
With a touch, impartially tender,
    On the blossoms blooming for all;
    Under the sod and the dew,
        Waiting the judgment day;—
    Broidered with gold, the Blue;
        Mellowed with gold, the Gray.

So, when the Summer calleth,
    On forest and field of grain
With an equal murmur falleth
    The cooling drip of the rain;—
    Under the sod and the dew,
        Waiting the judgment day;—
    Wet with the rain, the Blue;
        Wet with the rain, the Gray.

Sadly, but not with upbraiding,
    The generous deed was done;
In the storm of the years that are fading,
    No braver battle was won;—
    Under the sod and the dew,
        Waiting the judgment day;—
    Under the blossoms, the Blue,
        Under the garlands, the Gray.

No more shall the war-cry sever,
  Or the winding rivers be red;
They banish our anger forever
    When they laurel the graves of our dead!
      Under the sod and the dew,
        Waiting the judgment day;—
      Love and tears for the Blue,
        Tears and love for the Gray.

Ethnogenesis

Written during the meeting of the first Southern Congress,
at Montgomery, February, 1861.

I.

Hath not the morning dawned with added light?
And will not evening call another star
Out of the infinite regions of the night,
To mark this day in Heaven? At last, we are
A nation among nations; and the world
Shall soon behold in many a distant port
      Another Flag unfurled!
Now, come what may, whose favor need we court?
And, under God, whose thunder need we fear?
      Thank Him who placed us here
Beneath so kind a sky—the very sun
Takes part with us; and on our errands run
All breezes of the ocean; dew and rain
Do noiseless battle for us; and the Year,
And all the gentle daughters in her train,
March in our ranks, and in our service wield
      Long spears of golden grain!
A yellow blossom as her fairy shield,
June flings her azure banner to the wind,
    While in the order of their birth
Her sisters pass, and many an ample field

Grows white beneath their steps, till now, behold
Its endless sheets unfold
THE SNOW OF SOUTHERN SUMMERS! Let the earth
Rejoice! beneath those fleeces soft and warm
Our happy land shall sleep
In a repose as deep
As if we lay intrenched behind
Whole leagues of Russian ice and Arctic storm!

II.

And what if, mad with wrongs themselves have wrought,
In their own treachery caught,
By their own fears made bold,
And leagued with him of old,
Who long since in the limits of the North
Set up his evil throne, and warred with God—
What if, both mad and blinded in their rage,
Our foes should fling us down their mortal gage,
And with a hostile step profane our sod!
We shall not shrink, my brothers, but go forth
To meet them, marshalled by the Lord of Hosts,
And overshadowed by the mighty ghosts
Of Moultrie and of Eutaw—who shall foil
Auxiliars such as these? Nor these alone,
But every stock and stone
Shall help us: but the very soil,
And all the generous wealth it gives to toil,
And all for which we love our noble land,
Shall fight beside, and through us, sea and strand,
The heart of woman, and her hand,
Tree, fruit, and flower, and every influence,

Gentle, or grave, or grand;
    The winds in our defence
Shall seem to blow; to us the hills shall lend
    Their firmness and their calm;
And in our stiffened sinews we shall blend
    The strength of pine and palm!

III.

Nor would we shun the battle-ground,
    Though weak as we are strong;
Call up the clashing elements around,
    And test the right and wrong!
On one side, creeds that dare to teach
What Christ and Paul refrained to preach;
Codes built upon a broken pledge,
And Charity that whets a poniard's edge;
Fair schemes that leave the neighboring poor
To starve and shiver at the schemer's door,
While in the world's most liberal ranks enrolled,
He turns some vast philanthropy to gold;
Religion, taking every mortal form
But that a pure and Christian faith makes warm,
Where not to vile fanatic passion urged,
Or not in vague philosophies submerged,
Repulsive with all Pharisaic leaven,
And making laws to stay the laws of Heaven!
And on the other, scorn of sordid gain,
Unblemished honor, truth without a stain,
Faith, justice, reverence, charitable wealth,
And, for the poor and humble, laws which give,
Not the mean right to buy the right to live,
    But life, and home, and health!

To doubt the end were want of trust in God,
        Who, if he has decreed
    That we must pass a redder sea
Than that which rang to Miriam's holy glee,
        Will surely raise at need
        A Moses with his rod!

    IV.

But let our fears—if fears we have—be still,
And turn us to the future! Could we climb
Some mighty Alp, and view the coming time,
We should indeed behold a sight to fill
        Our eyes with happy tears!
Not for the glories which a hundred years
Shall bring us; not for lands from sea to sea,
And wealth, and power, and peace, though these shall be;
But for the distant peoples we shall bless,
And the hushed murmurs of a world's distress:
For, to give labor to the poor,
        The whole sad planet o'er,
And save from want and crime the humblest door,
Is one among the many ends for which
        God makes us great and rich!
The hour perchance is not yet wholly ripe
When all shall own it, but the type
Whereby we shall be known in every land
Is that vast gulf which laves our Southern strand,
And through the cold, untempered ocean pours
Its genial streams, that far off Arctic shores
May sometimes catch upon the softened breeze
Strange tropic warmth and hints of summer seas.

Carolina

I.

The despot treads thy sacred sands,
Thy pines give shelter to his bands,
Thy sons stand by with idle hands,
    Carolina!
He breathes at ease thy airs of balm,
He scorns the lances of thy palm;
Oh! who shall break thy craven calm,
    Carolina!
Thy ancient fame is growing dim,
A spot is on thy garment's rim,
Give to the winds thy battle hymn,
    Carolina!

II.

Call on thy children of the hill,
Wake swamp and river, coast and rill,
Rouse all thy strength and all thy skill,
    Carolina!
Cite wealth and science, trade and art,
Touch with thy fire the cautious mart,
And pour thee through the people's heart,
    Carolina!
Till even the coward spurns his fears,
And all thy fields and fens and meres,
Shall bristle like thy palm with spears,
    Carolina!

III.

Hold up the glories of thy dead;
Say how thy elder children bled,
And point to Eutaw's battle-bed,
                    Carolina!
Tell how the patriot's soul was tried,
And what his dauntless breast defied;
How Rutledge ruled and Laurens died,
                    Carolina!
Cry! till thy summons, heard at last,
Shall fall like Marion's bugle blast
Re-echoed from the haunted Past,
                    Carolina!

IV.

I hear a murmur as of waves
That grope their way through sunless caves,
Like bodies struggling in their graves,
                    Carolina!
And now it deepens; slow and grand
It swells, as rolling to the land
An ocean broke upon the strand,
                    Carolina!
Shout! let it reach the startled Huns!
And roar with all thy festal guns!
It is the answer of thy sons,
                    Carolina!

V.

They will not wait to hear thee call;
From Sachem's head to Sumter's wall

Resounds the voice of hut and hall,
                    Carolina!
No! thou hast not a stain they say,
Or none save what the battle-day
Shall wash in seas of blood away,
                    Carolina!
Thy skirts indeed the foe may part,
Thy robe be pierced with sword and dart,
They shall not touch thy noble heart,
                    Carolina!

VI.

Ere thou shalt own the tyrant's thrall
Ten times ten thousand men must fall;
Thy corpse may hearken to his call,
                    Carolina!
When by thy bier in mournful throngs
The women chant thy mortal wrongs,
'T will be their own funereal songs,
                    Carolina!
From thy dead breast by ruffians trod
No helpless child shall look to God;
All shall be safe beneath thy sod,
                    Carolina!

VII.

Girt with such wills to do and bear,
Assured in right, and mailed in prayer,
Thou wilt not bow thee to despair,
                    Carolina!
Throw thy bold banner to the breeze!

Front with thy ranks the threatening seas
Like thine own proud armorial trees,
                    Carolina!
Fling down thy gauntlet to the Huns,
And roar the challenge from thy guns;
Then leave the future to thy sons,
                    Carolina!

Charleston

Calm as that second summer which precedes
    The first fall of the snow,
In the broad sunlight of heroic deeds,
    The City bides the foe.

As yet, behind their ramparts stern and proud,
    Her bolted thunders sleep—
Dark Sumter, like a battlemented cloud,
    Looms o'er the solemn deep.

No Calpe frowns from lofty cliff or scar
    To guard the holy strand;
But Moultrie holds in leash her dogs of war
    Above the level sand.

And down the dunes a thousand guns lie couched,
    Unseen, beside the flood—
Like tigers in some Orient jungle crouched
    That wait and watch for blood.

Meanwhile, through streets still echoing with trade,
   Walk grave and thoughtful men,
Whose hands may one day wield the patriot's blade
   As lightly as the pen.

And maidens, with such eyes as would grow dim
   Over a bleeding hound,
Seem each one to have caught the strength of him
   Whose sword she sadly bound.

Thus girt without and garrisoned at home,
   Day patient following day,
Old Charleston looks from roof, and spire, and dome,
   Across her tranquil bay.

Ships, through a hundred foes, from Saxon lands
   And spicy Indian ports,
Bring Saxon steel and iron to her hands,
   And summer to her courts.

But still, along yon dim Atlantic line,
   The only hostile smoke
Creeps like a harmless mist above the brine,
   From some frail, floating oak.

Shall the spring dawn, and she still clad in smiles,
   And with an unscathed brow,
Rest in the strong arms of her palm-crowned isles,
   As fair and free as now?

We know not; in the temple of the Fates
    God has inscribed her doom;
And, all untroubled in her faith, she waits
    The triumph or the tomb.

Carmen Triumphale

Go forth and bid the land rejoice,
    Yet not too gladly, O my song!
    Breathe softly, as if mirth would wrong
The solemn rapture of thy voice.

Be nothing lightly done or said
    This happy day! Our joy should flow
    Accordant with the lofty woe
That wails above the noble dead.

Let him whose brow and breast were calm
    While yet the battle lay with God,
    Look down upon the crimson sod
And gravely wear his mournful palm;

And him, whose heart still weak from fear
    Beats all too gayly for the time,
    Know that intemperate glee is crime
While one dead hero claims a tear.

Yet go thou forth, my song! and thrill,
    With sober joy, the troubled days;
    A nation's hymn of grateful praise
May not be hushed for private ill.

Our foes are fallen! Flash, ye wires!
   The mighty tidings far and nigh!
   Ye cities! write them on the sky
In purple and in emerald fires!

They came with many a haughty boast;
   Their threats were heard on every breeze;
   They darkened half the neighboring seas,
And swooped like vultures on the coast.

False recreants in all knightly strife,
   Their way was wet with woman's tears;
   Behind them flamed the toil of years,
And bloodshed stained the sheaves of life.

They fought as tyrants fight, or slaves;
   God gave the dastards to our hands;
   Their bones are bleaching on the sands,
Or mouldering slow in shallow graves.

What though we hear about our path
   The heavens with howls of vengeance rent?
   The venom of their hate is spent;
We need not heed their fangless wrath.

Meantime the stream they strove to chain
   Now drinks a thousand springs, and sweeps
   With broadening breast, and mightier deeps,
And rushes onward to the main!

While down the swelling current glides
    Our Ship of State before the blast,
    With streamers poured from every mast,
Her thunders roaring from her sides.

Lord! bid the frenzied tempest cease,
    Hang out thy rainbow on the sea!
    Laugh round her, waves! in silver glee,
And speed her to the ports of peace!

The Unknown Dead

The rain is plashing on my sill,
But all the winds of Heaven are still;
And so it falls with that dull sound
Which thrills us in the church-yard ground,
When the first spadeful drops like lead
Upon the coffin of the dead.
Beyond my streaming window-pane,
I cannot see the neighboring vane,
Yet from its old familiar tower
The bell comes, muffled, through the shower.
What strange and unsuspected link
Of feeling touched, has made me think—
While with a vacant soul and eye
I watch that gray and stony sky—
Of nameless graves on battle-plains
Washed by a single winter's rains,
Where, some beneath Virginian hills,

And some by green Atlantic rills,
Some by the waters of the West,
A myriad unknown heroes rest.
Ah! not the chiefs who, dying, see
Their flags in front of victory,
Or, at their life-blood's noble cost
Pay for a battle nobly lost,
Claim from their monumental beds
The bitterest tears a nation sheds.
Beneath yon lonely mound—the spot
By all save some fond few forgot—
Lie the true martyrs of the fight
Which strikes for freedom and for right.
Of them, their patriot zeal and pride,
The lofty faith that with them died,
No grateful page shall farther tell
Than that so many bravely fell;
And we can only dimly guess
What worlds of all this world's distress,
What utter woe, despair, and dearth,
Their fate has brought to many a hearth.
Just such a sky as this should weep
Above them, always, where they sleep;
Yet, haply, at this very hour,
Their graves are like a lover's bower;
And Nature's self, with eyes unwet,
Oblivious of the crimson debt
To which she owes her April grace,
Laughs gayly o'er their burial place.

Lines

Sleep sweetly in your humble graves,
   Sleep martyrs of a fallen cause!—
Though yet no marble column craves
   The pilgrim here to pause.

In seeds of laurels in the earth,
   The garlands of your fame are sown;
And, somewhere, waiting for its birth,
   The shaft is in the stone.

Meanwhile, your sisters for the years
   Which hold in trust your storied tombs,
Bring all they now can give you—tears,
   And these memorial blooms.

Small tributes, but your shades will smile
   As proudly on those wreaths to-day,
As when some cannon-moulded pile
   Shall overlook this Bay.

Stoop angels hither from the skies!
   There is no holier spot of ground,
Than where defeated valor lies
   By mourning beauty crowned.

A Soldier's Letter

January 20, 1862.

With the head of a drum for my desk, I sit on a southern
slope,
    While the sunlight streaks the apples that hang in the
orchard hard by,
And puzzle my brains over verses and many a
marvellous trope,
    And vainly seek inspiration from out the sky.
What can I tell you now that you have not known
before?
    How dearly I love you, Mary, and how hard the
parting was,
And how bravely you kissed my lips when we stood at
the open door,
    And blessed me for going with heart and hand in the
cause!
O, sweet as a lily flushed with the red of the roses near
    When beat by the hot, implacable sun above,
Was the hue of your angel face, as tear after tear
    Rose to your ivory eyelids and welled with love!

War is not quite so hard as you poor townspeople think;
    We have plenty of food to eat, and a good, warm
blanket at night,
And now and then, you know, a quiet, moderate drink;

Which doesn't hurt us, dearest, and makes things
        right.
But the greatest blessing of all is the total want of care;
    The happy, complete reliance of the carefully-
        guardianed child
Who has no thought for his dinner, and is given good
        clothes to wear,
    And whose leisure moments are with innocent sports
        beguiled.
The drill of the soldier is pleasant, if one works with a
        willing heart,
    It is only the worthless fellow that grumbles at double-
        quick;
I like the ingenious manœuvres that constitute war an
        art,
    And not even the cleaning of arms can make me sick.

One of the comrades five that sleep in the tent with me
    Is a handsome, fair-faced boy, with curling, sun-
        burned hair;
Like me, he has left a sweetheart on the shore of the
        northern sea,
    And, like her I love, he says she also is good and fair.
So we talk of our girls at night when the other chaps are
        asleep,—
    Talk in the sacred whispers that are low with the
        choke of love,—
And often when we are silent I think I can hear him
        weep,

And murmur her name in accents that croon like the
nesting dove.
Then, when we are out on picket, and the nights are
calm and still,
When our beats lie close together, we pause and chat-
ter the same;
And the weary hours pass swiftly, till over the distant hill
The sun comes up unclouded and fierce with flame.

The scene that I look on is lovely! The cotton-fields
smooth and white,
With the bending negroes shelling the flocculent,
bursting pods,
And the quiet sentinels slowly pacing the neighboring
height,
And now and then hidden by groups of the golden-
rods.
Beautiful are the isles that mottle the slumberous bay;
Beautiful are the azure veins of the creeks;
Beautiful is the crimson that, far away,
Burns on the woods like the paint on an Indian's
cheeks!
Beautiful are the thoughts of the time when— Hist!
What sound is that I hear? 'T is the rifle's continuous
crack!
The long-roll beats to arms! I must not—cannot be
missed.
Dear love, I'll finish this letter when I come back.

Don't be startled, my darling, at this handwriting not
      being mine:
  I have been a little ill, and the comrade I spoke of
      before
Has kindly offered to take from my loving lips this line;
  So he holds, as you see, the pen I can hold no more.
That was a skirmish that came, as I wrote to you, out on
      the hill;
  We had sharp fighting a while, and I lost my arm.
There! don't cry, my darling!—it will not kill,
  And other poor fellows there met greater harm.
I have my left arm still to fold you close to my heart,
  All the strength of my lost one will pass into that, I
      know;
We soon shall be together, never, never to part,
  And to suffer thus for your country is bliss, not woe!

SILAS WEIR MITCHELL | 1829–1914

How the Cumberland Went Down

Gray swept the angry waves
   O'er the gallant and the true,
Rolled high in mounded graves
   O'er the stately frigate's crew—
Over cannon, over deck,
Over all that ghastly wreck,—
      When the Cumberland went down.

Such a roar the waters rent
   As though a giant died,
When the wailing billows went
   Above those heroes tried;
And the sheeted foam leaped high,
Like white ghosts against the sky,—
      As the Cumberland went down.

O shrieking waves that gushed
   Above that loyal band,
Your cold, cold burial rushed
   O'er many a heart on land!
And from all the startled North
A cry of pain broke forth,
      When the Cumberland went down.

And forests old, that gave
   A thousand years of power
To her lordship of the wave
   And her beauty's regal dower,
Bent, as though before a blast,
When plunged her pennoned mast,
     And the Cumberland went down.

And grimy mines that sent
   To her their virgin strength,
And iron vigor lent
   To knit her lordly length,
Wildly stirred with throbs of life,
Echoes of that fatal strife,
     As the Cumberland went down.

Beneath the ocean vast,
   Full many a captain bold,
By many a rotting mast,
   And admiral of old,
Rolled restless in his grave
As he felt the sobbing wave,
     When the Cumberland went down.

And stern Vikings that lay
   A thousand years at rest,
In many a deep blue bay
   Beneath the Baltic's breast,
Leaped on the silver sands,
And shook their rusty brands,
     As the Cumberland went down.

1862

Of Bronze – and Blaze –
The North – tonight –
So adequate – it forms –
So preconcerted with itself –
So distant – to alarms –
An Unconcern so sovreign
To Universe, or me –
Infects my simple spirit
With Taints of Majesty –
Till I take vaster attitudes –
And strut upon my stem –
Disdaining Men, and Oxygen,
For Arrogance of them –

My Splendors, are Menagerie –
But their Competeless Show
Will entertain the Centuries
When I, am long ago,
An Island in dishonored Grass –
Whom none but Daisies, know –

If any sink, assure that this, now standing –
Failed like Themselves – and conscious that it rose –
Grew by the Fact, and not the Understanding
How Weakness passed – or Force – arose –

Tell that the Worst, is easy in a Moment –
Dread, but the Whizzing, before the Ball –
When the Ball enters, enters Silence –
Dying – annuls the power to kill –

It feels a shame to be Alive –
When Men so brave – are dead –
One envies the Distinguished Dust –
Permitted – such a Head –

The Stone – that tells defending Whom
This Spartan put away
What little of Him we – possessed
In Pawn for Liberty –

The price is great – Sublimely paid –
Do we deserve – a Thing –
That lives – like Dollars – must be piled
Before we may obtain?

Are we that wait – sufficient worth –
That such Enormous Pearl
As life – dissolved be – for Us –
In Battle's – horrid Bowl?

It may be – a Renown to live –
I think the Men who die –
Those unsustained – Saviors –
Present Divinity –

———

When I was small, a Woman died –
Today – her Only Boy
Went up from the Potomac –
His face all Victory

To look at her – How slowly
The Seasons must have turned
Till Bullets clipt an Angle
And He passed quickly round –

If pride shall be in Paradise –
Ourself cannot decide –
Of their imperial conduct –
No person testified –

But, proud in Apparition –
That Woman and her Boy
Pass back and forth, before my Brain
As even in the sky –

I'm confident, that Bravoes –
Perpetual break abroad
For Braveries, remote as this
In Yonder Maryland –

———

My Portion is Defeat – today –
A paler luck than Victory –
Less Paeans – fewer Bells –
The Drums dont follow Me – with tunes –
Defeat – a somewhat slower – means –
More Arduous than Balls –

'Tis populous with Bone and stain –
And Men too straight to stoop again –
And Piles of solid Moan –
And Chips of Blank – in Boyish Eyes –
And scraps of Prayer –
And Death's surprise,
Stamped visible – in stone –

There's somewhat prouder, Over there –
The Trumpets tell it to the Air –
How different Victory
To Him who has it – and the One
Who to have had it, would have been
Contenteder – to die –

He fought like those Who've nought to lose –
Bestowed Himself to Balls
As One who for a further Life
Had not a further Use –

Invited Death – with bold attempt –
But Death was Coy of Him
As Other Men, were Coy of Death.
To Him – to live – was Doom –

His Comrades, shifted like the Flakes
When Gusts reverse the Snow –
But He – was left alive Because
Of Greediness to die –

PAUL HAMILTON HAYNE | 1830–1886

Vicksburg—A Ballad

For sixty days and upwards,
　A storm of shell and shot
Rained round us in a flaming shower,
　But still we faltered not.
"If the noble city perish,"
　Our grand young leader said,
"Let the only walls the foe shall scale
　"Be ramparts of the dead!"

For sixty days and upwards,
　The eye of heaven waxed dim;
And e'en throughout God's holy morn,
　O'er Christian prayer and hymn,
Arose a hissing tumult,
　As if the fiends in air
Strove to engulf the voice of faith
　In the shrieks of their despair.

There was wailing in the houses,
　There was trembling on the marts,
While the tempest raged and thundered,
　'Mid the silent thrill of hearts;
But the Lord, our shield, was with us,
　And ere a month had sped,

Our very women walked the streets
   With scarce one throb of dread.

And the little children gambolled,
   Their faces purely raised,
Just for a wondering moment,
   As the huge bombs whirled and blazed,
Then turned with silvery laughter
   To the sports which children love,
Thrice-mailed in the sweet, instinctive thought
   That the good God watched above.

Yet the hailing bolts fell faster,
   From scores of flame-clad ships,
And about us, denser, darker,
   Grew the conflict's wild eclipse,
Till a solid cloud closed o'er us,
   Like a type of doom and ire,
Whence shot a thousand quivering tongues
   Of forked and vengeful fire.

But the unseen hands of angels
   Those death-shafts warned aside,
And the dove of heavenly mercy
   Ruled o'er the battle tide;
In the houses ceased the wailing,
   And through the war-scarred marts
The people strode, with step of hope,
   To the music in their hearts.

AUGUSTA COOPER BRISTOL | 1835–1910

The Crime of the Ages

1861

Poet, write!
Not of a purpose dark and dire,
That souls of evil fashion,
Nor the power that nerves the assassin's hand,
In the white heat of his passion:
But let thy rhyme,
Through every clime,
A burthen bear of this one crime:
Let the world draw in a shuddering breath,
O'er the crime that aims at a nation's death!

Minstrel, sing!
Not in affection's dulcet tone,
Or with sound of a soft recorder:
Strike not thy harp to a strain arranged
In measured, harmonic order:
But loud and strong
The tones prolong,
That thunder of a Nation's wrong;
Let a sound of war in thy notes appear,
Till the world opes wide a startled ear!

Soldier, fight!
Thou hast a patriot's throbbing pulse,
And future history's pages,
Shall tell of the blood so freely shed
To redeem "the crime of the ages."
Well may'st thou fight
For Truth and Right,
And teach a rebel foe thy might!
Let a loyal heart, and undaunted will,
Show the world we are a Nation still!

Prophet, speak!
Speak for the children of martyred sires,
An offspring the most ungrateful!
Warn them of Justice hurrying on,
To punish a deed so hateful!
O read with thy
Prophetic eye,
The omens of our troubled sky!
What is the picture beyond the gloom?
New life, new birth, or a Nation's tomb?

THOMAS BAILEY ALDRICH | 1836–1907

Fredericksburg

The increasing moonlight drifts across my bed,
And on the churchyard by the road, I know
It falls as white and noiselessly as snow. . . .
'T was such a night two weary summers fled;
The stars, as now, were waning overhead.
Listen! Again the shrill-lipped bugles blow
Where the swift currents of the river flow
Past Fredericksburg; far off the heavens are red
With sudden conflagration; on yon height,
Linstock in hand, the gunners hold their breath;
A signal rocket pierces the dense night,
Flings its spent stars upon the town beneath:
Hark!—the artillery massing on the right,
Hark!—the black squadrons wheeling down to Death!

By the Potomac

The soft new grass is creeping o'er the graves
By the Potomac; and the crisp ground-flower
Tilts its blue cup to catch the passing shower;
The pine-cone ripens, and the long moss waves
Its tangled gonfalons above our braves.
Hark, what a burst of music from yon bower!—
The Southern nightingale that hour by hour
In its melodious summer madness raves.
Ah, with what delicate touches of her hand,
With what sweet voice of bird and rivulet
And drowsy murmur of the rustling leaf
Would Nature soothe us, bidding us forget
The awful crime of this distracted land
And all our heavy heritage of grief.

John Burns of Gettysburg

Have you heard the story that gossips tell
Of Burns of Gettysburg?—No? Ah, well:
Brief is the glory that hero earns,
Briefer the story of poor John Burns:
He was the fellow who won renown,—
The only man who didn't back down
When the rebels rode through his native town:
But held his own in the fight next day,
When all his townsfolk ran away.
That was in July, sixty-three,
The very day that General Lee,
Flower of Southern chivalry,
Baffled and beaten, backward reeled
From a stubborn Meade and a barren field.

I might tell how, but the day before,
John Burns stood at his cottage door,
Looking down the village street,
Where, in the shade of his peaceful vine,
He heard the low of his gathered kine,
And felt their breath with incense sweet;
Or I might say, when the sunset burned
The old farm gable, he thought it turned
The milk that fell, in a babbling flood

Into the milk-pail, red as blood!
Or how he fancied the hum of bees
Were bullets buzzing among the trees.
But all such fanciful thoughts as these
Were strange to a practical man like Burns,
Who minded only his own concerns,
Troubled no more by fancies fine
Than one of his calm-eyed, long-tailed kine,—
Quite old-fashioned and matter-of-fact,
Slow to argue, but quick to act.
That was the reason, as some folk say,
He fought so well on that terrible day.

And it was terrible. On the right
Raged for hours the heady fight,
Thundered the battery's double bass,—
Difficult music for men to face;
While on the left—where now the graves
Undulate like the living waves
That all that day unceasing swept
Up to the pits the rebels kept—
Round shot ploughed the upland glades,
Sown with bullets, reaped with blades;
Shattered fences here and there
Tossed their splinters in the air;
The very trees were stripped and bare;
The barns that once held yellow grain
Were heaped with harvests of the slain;
The cattle bellowed on the plain,
The turkeys screamed with might and main,
And brooding barn-fowl left their rest
With strange shells bursting in each nest.

Just where the tide of battle turns,
Erect and lonely stood old John Burns.
How do you think the man was dressed?
He wore an ancient long buff vest,
Yellow as saffron,—but his best;
And, buttoned over his manly breast,
Was a bright blue coat, with a rolling collar,
And large gilt buttons,—size of a dollar,—
With tails that the country-folk called "swaller."
He wore a broad-brimmed, bell-crowned hat,
White as the locks on which it sat.
Never had such a sight been seen
For forty years on the village green,
Since old John Burns was a country beau,
And went to the "quiltings" long ago.

Close at his elbows all that day,
Veterans of the Peninsula,
Sunburnt and bearded, charged away;
And striplings, downy of lip and chin,—
Clerks that the Home Guard mustered in,—
Glanced, as they passed, at the hat he wore,
Then at the rifle his right hand bore;
And hailed him, from out their youthful lore,
With scraps of a slangy *répertoire*:
"How are you, White Hat!" "Put her through!"
"Your head's level," and "Bully for you!"
Called him "Daddy,"—begged he'd disclose
The name of the tailor who made his clothes,
And what was the value he set on those;
While Burns, unmindful of jeer and scoff,
Stood there picking the rebels off,—

With his long brown rifle, and bell-crown hat,
And the swallow-tails they were laughing at.

'T was but a moment, for that respect
Which clothes all courage their voices checked;
And something the wildest could understand
Spake in the old man's strong right hand;
And his corded throat, and the lurking frown
Of his eyebrows under his old bell-crown;
Until, as they gazed, there crept an awe
Through the ranks in whispers, and some men saw
In the antique vestments and long white hair,
The Past of the Nation in battle there;
And some of the soldiers since declare
That the gleam of his old white hat afar,
Like the crested plume of the brave Navarre,
That day was their oriflamme of war.

So raged the battle. You know the rest:
How the rebels, beaten and backward pressed,
Broke at the final charge, and ran.
At which John Burns—a practical man—
Shouldered his rifle, unbent his brows,
And then went back to his bees and cows.

That is the story of old John Burns;
This is the moral the reader learns:
In fighting the battle, the question's whether
You'll show a hat that's white, or a feather!

Relieving Guard

T.S.K. Obiit March 4, 1864.

Came the Relief. "What, Sentry, ho!
How passed the night through thy long waking?"
"Cold, cheerless, dark,—as may befit
The hour before the dawn is breaking."

"No sight? no sound?" "No; nothing save
The plover from the marshes calling,
And in yon Western sky, about
An hour ago, a Star was falling."

"A star? There's nothing strange in that."
"No, nothing; but, above the thicket,
Somehow it seemed to me that God
Somewhere had just relieved a picket."

A Second Review of the Grand Army

I read last night of the grand review
In Washington's chiefest avenue,—
Two hundred thousand men in blue,
    I think they said was the number,—
Till I seemed to hear their trampling feet,
The bugle blast and the drum's quick beat,
The clatter of hoofs in the stony street,
The cheers of people who came to greet,
And the thousand details that to repeat

Would only my verse encumber,—
Till I fell in a reverie, sad and sweet,
    And then to a fitful slumber.

When, lo! in a vision I seemed to stand
In the lonely Capitol. On each hand
Far stretched the portico, dim and grand
Its columns ranged like a martial band
Of sheeted spectres, whom some command
    Had called to a last reviewing.
And the streets of the city were white and bare;
No footfall echoed across the square;
But out of the misty midnight air
I heard in the distance a trumpet blare,
And the wandering night-winds seemed to bear
    The sound of a far tattooing.

Then I held my breath with fear and dread;
For into the square, with a brazen tread,
There rode a figure whose stately head
    O'erlooked the review that morning,
That never bowed from its firm-set seat
When the living column passed its feet,
Yet now rode steadily up the street
    To the phantom bugle's warning:

Till it reached the Capitol square, and wheeled,
And there in the moonlight stood revealed
A well-known form that in State and field
    Had led our patriot sires:
Whose face was turned to the sleeping camp,

Afar through the river's fog and damp,
That showed no flicker, nor waning lamp,
    Nor wasted bivouac fires.

And I saw a phantom army come,
With never a sound of fife or drum,
But keeping time to a throbbing hum
    Of wailing and lamentation:
The martyred heroes of Malvern Hill,
Of Gettysburg and Chancellorsville,
The men whose wasted figures fill
    The patriot graves of the nation.

And there came the nameless dead,—the men
Who perished in fever swamp and fen,
The slowly-starved of the prison pen;
    And, marching beside the others,
Came the dusky martyrs of Pillow's fight,
With limbs enfranchised and bearing bright;
I thought—perhaps 't was the pale moonlight—
    They looked as white as their brothers!

And so all night marched the nation's dead,
With never a banner above them spread,
Nor a badge, nor a motto brandishèd;
No mark—save the bare uncovered head
    Of the silent bronze Reviewer;
With never an arch save the vaulted sky;
With never a flower save those that lie
On the distant graves—for love could buy
    No gift that was purer or truer.

So all night long swept the strange array,
So all night long till the morning gray
I watched for one who had passed away;
    With a reverent awe and wonder,—
Till a blue cap waved in the length'ning line,
And I knew that one who was kin of mine
Had come; and I spake—and lo! that sign
    Awakened me from my slumber.

The Sword of Robert Lee

Forth from its scabbard, pure and bright,
    Flashed the sword of Lee!
Far in the front of the deadly fight,
High o'er the brave in the cause of Right,
Its stainless sheen, like a beacon light,
    Led us to Victory.

Out of its scabbard, where, full long,
    It slumbered peacefully,
Roused from its rest by the battle's song,
Shielding the feeble, smiting the strong,
Guarding the right, avenging the wrong,
    Gleamed the sword of Lee.

Forth from its scabbard, high in air
    Beneath Virginia's sky—
And they who saw it gleaming there,
And knew who bore it, knelt to swear
That where that sword led they would dare
    To follow—and to die.

Out of its scabbard! Never hand
    Waved sword from stain as free,
Nor purer sword led braver band,

Nor braver bled for a brighter land,
Nor brighter land had a cause so grand,
Nor cause a chief like Lee!

Forth from its scabbard! How we prayed
That sword might victor be;
And when our triumph was delayed,
And many a heart grew sore afraid,
We still hoped on while gleamed the blade
Of noble Robert Lee.

Forth from its scabbard all in vain
Bright flashed the sword of Lee;
'Tis shrouded now in its sheath again,
It sleeps the sleep of our noble slain,
Defeated, yet without a stain,
Proudly and peacefully.

Maryland

The despot's heel is on thy shore,
    Maryland!
His torch is at thy temple door,
    Maryland!
Avenge the patriotic gore
That flecked the streets of Baltimore,
And be the battle-queen of yore,
    Maryland! My Maryland!

Hark to a wand'ring son's appeal,
    Maryland!
My mother State! to thee I kneel,
    Maryland!
For life and death, for woe and weal,
Thy peerless chivalry reveal,
And gird thy beauteous limbs with steel,
    Maryland! My Maryland!

Thou wilt not cower in the dust,
    Maryland!
Thy beaming sword shall never rust,
    Maryland!
Remember Carroll's sacred trust,
Remember Howard's warlike thrust—

And all thy slumberers with the just,
     Maryland! My Maryland!

Come! 'tis the red dawn of the day,
     Maryland!
Come! with thy panoplied array,
     Maryland!
With Ringgold's spirit for the fray,
With Watson's blood at Monterey,
With fearless Lowe and dashing May,
     Maryland! My Maryland!

Come! for thy shield is bright and strong,
     Maryland!
Come! for thy dalliance does thee wrong,
     Maryland!
Come! to thine own heroic throng,
That stalks with Liberty along,
And give a new *Key* to thy song,
     Maryland! My Maryland!

Dear Mother! burst the tyrant's chain,
     Maryland!
Virginia should not call in vain,
     Maryland!
She meets her sisters on the plain—
"*Sic semper*," 'tis the proud refrain,
That baffles minions back amain,
     Maryland!
Arise, in majesty again,
     Maryland! My Maryland!

I see the blush upon thy cheek,
        Maryland!
But thou wast ever bravely meek,
        Maryland!
But lo! there surges forth a shriek
From hill to hill, from creek to creek—
Potomac calls to Chesapeake,
        Maryland! My Maryland!

Thou wilt not yield the Vandal toll,
        Maryland!
Thou wilt not crook to his control,
        Maryland!
Better the fire upon thee roll,
Better the blade, the shot, the bowl,
Than crucifixion of the soul,
        Maryland! My Maryland!

I hear the distant thunder-hum,
        Maryland!
The Old Line's bugle, fife and drum,
        Maryland!
She is not dead, nor deaf, nor dumb—
Huzza! she spurns the Northern scum!
She breathes—she burns! she'll come! she'll come!
        Maryland! My Maryland!

NATHANIEL SOUTHGATE SHALER | 1841–1906

Near the Front

A street in country town at midnight time:
Above, the harvest moon; below, the earth
War-stricken, desolate. On either side
Is utter ruin; here, by flame that left
But whitened remnants,—there, yet sorrier
In shops and dwellings where the doors stand wide
And trampled goods tell plain that plunderers
Have ravaged where men stored. Along this street
Is laid a hard-marched column by its arms:
Close-packed upon the sidewalks, with the feet
In dusty gutters and each side the way
Crammed close as herring in a box; they sleep
With breasts to sky or earth: shaped as they'll lie
Within the trenches ere the shovelers
Have done their part. Upon the unblocked road,
Six paces wide, pass on the endless trains
Of laden wagons, guns, and cavalry
To hard-pressed front: and a like ceaseless line
Of ambulances bearing to the rear
Their loads of misery. The creaking wheels
Crunch on the loosened stones two feet away
From outer lines of heads, and send the dust
Upon their senseless eyes. The riders sway
Nigh out their saddles and the horses lean

One 'gainst the other as they stumble on,
For they, too, slumber—yea, this world's asleep,
Save from each ambulance the wounded tell
They know their torment. There one pleads for drink—
Poor chap, his bandage's loosened and he thirsts
Because his life flows out. He'll soon be still:
His cry is but a quaver; he'll soon slake
Thirst at the eternal spring. See, there goes
A woman treading softly through the host,
Scanning the faces upturned to the sky
With eager stealth. Swift glance and then swift on
Until she's out of sight.

The Marksman's Work

                  The silent lines
Are set against each other in the pause
That comes before the battle; watching near
The chance of stroke and parry. Waiting still
For some last vantage of new men, or guns,
Or for belated scouts who search the point
Where well-aimed blow may tell. It is a time
When soul is tense as bowstring with its shaft
Down to the head: when all the leaders watch
As cats before the pounce.
                  In front of us
Are fields whereon for half a mile there is
No note of what's to come. The sheep feed there,
As by the shambles they are wont to crop

What good earth sends of nurture. But away
Nigh thousand yards beyond our outer force,
Are foemen's pickets: on their line a house,
The homestead of these fields, and by its side,
Beneath an orchard's shade, a battery
Where men lie by their guns, while right and left
Stretches the dun line of their waiting host.
Upon the housetop, seated on the crest,
There sits a soldier, bending o'er a board,
Making a sketch-map of our front. We see
With the unaided eye no more than this,
For in that distance man is but a mite—
Mere fleck 'gainst earth or sky. Yet with the glass
We change him to near neighbour. So we find
He is an officer, fair-shaped and young,
Who's deftly at his task. Now he looks up,
And with hand-shaded eyes he scans our front:
Then with his pencil turns them to his sketch.
It is a pretty sight, as innocent
As the sheep cropping in the quiet field,
And yet he knows 't is venture, hardiest
A man may make in war, and we know well
He is a brave man whom we needs must slay
So swift we can.

       Quick the commander calls—
"Here, Captain, have a gun with your best squad
And knock that fellow off."

           "It shall be done.
But you should see that close beside that house
They have a battery, and to my gun
They're sure to send an answer from their own;

And then the dance begins."

"We don't want that,
Yet we must stop that rascal."

"Let me call
A fellow from the regiment that serves
As my support. He is the crackest shot
From Minnesota: used to just such work
In potting redskins."

"Have him for a try—
Nine hundred yards—I'll bet a hat he'll miss,
Yet it is worth the trying, for the ball
May scare the villain off."

Up comes the man,
A lank and grizzled fellow, with the eye,
Blue-grey and strangely steadfast, of the sort
Who have the slaying habit. "Can you hit
That chap upon the housetop?"

"Guess I can,
It is a long shot, but there ain't no wind."

Slowly he loads his rifle; then he goes
Down to a fence; looks long and silently
As if he paced the distance in his mind:
Now lies upon his belly; finds a rest
To hold his piece that suits him, by a post.
We see him ready, and with glass to eyes
A score watch for the end. There sits the youth,
The picture of an artist at his task,
Outgoing to the world and bringing back
Share of its wealth. How happy he seems there
In the new morning! *Crack!* the rifle rings:
We hold breath for an instant. There he goes
Backward behind the ridgepole, while his sketch

Flits down the roof towards us. As the face
Slips out of sight, we see the startled look
That comes upon it when the man knows death.
We close our glasses; not a word is said;
The marksman stalks away; he does not look
Into our eyes, but straightway on: and we
Keep eyes from others' faces and seek out
Some trifling thing to do.

The Merry Truce

Over against each other lie the lines.
It's winter in the South, and that means mud
Knee-deep in roads and fields. So now the men
Squat round the smudging camp-fires and wait on
For the good Lord to send an earth that fits
For Satan's work: until the glorious sun
Shall shoot the thrill of spring deep in the ground
And shape the footing, so that men may tread
The ways of war. They while away the days
In idle jokes alike on friends and foes.
They are right neighbourly: the pickets play
Old sledge together; have their swapping trades,
And yarns of what they've done, and what they'll do
When springtime comes again.—And when there comes
A flag of truce, 't is a red-letter day
For those who bear it forth, while those who stay
Can gossip of its purpose for a week.
This morning one goes forth. Our general's heard
That his old father's ill. His enemy,

House friend and schoolmate, kinsman of degree,
Who leads the Yanks, will have the news from home.
So ra-ta-ta of bugles and a pole
With rag atop gives right to cross the field
Between the outposts to the foeman's lines,
And have an hour's chaff. Their general
Gives kindly welcome, grave, a bit reserved,
As fits a flag of truce, and better yet
A breakfast to the escort. Rules of war
Are set against such grace, for you should keep
Your foeman's belly empty for the chance
Swifter to smite him down. But those who bear
A white flag are good friends while it is up,
On mutual business bent, and so they claim
The mess right with you. Now comes idle talk
Of swapping prisoners, of sundry mules
A widow's lost and Federal scouts have found;
Then to the pith of it—the old man's health.
He is reported better, nigh to well,
But sore borne down with sorrow that his son
Is a damned Rebel. For yet other news
Our host sends with his compliments a jug
Unto our leader, knowing it will give
Some further consolation to his mate.
Back comes the flag again, then, Ra-ta-ta
And it is lowered. Foes we are again.
The pickets are alert, for well they know
That after truce there's apt to be a row.
There's nothing but a racket in the tent
Of our good leader—on until the morn.
Again the flag of truce climbs o'er the field,
With his regards and very earnest prayer
For further news from Frankfort.

Thomas at Chickamauga

It was that fierce contested field when Chickamauga lay
Beneath the wild tornado that swept her pride away;
Her dimpling dales and circling hills dyed crimson with
the flood
That had its sources in the springs that throb with
human blood.

"Go say to General Harker to reinforce his right!"
Said Thomas to his *aide-de-camp*, when wildly went the
fight;
In front the battle thundered, it roared both right and
left,
But like a rock "Pap" Thomas stood upon the crested
cleft.

"Where will I find you, General, when I return?" The aide
Leaned on his bridle-rein to wait the answer Thomas
made;
The old chief like a lion turned, his pale lips set and
sere,
And shook his mane, and stamped his foot, and fiercely
answered, *"Here!"*

The floodtide of fraternal strife rolled upward to his
feet,

And like the breakers on the shore the thunderous
    clamors beat;
The sad earth rocked and reeled with woe, the
    woodland shrieked in pain,
And hill and vale were groaning with the burden of the
    slain.

Who does not mind that sturdy form, that steady heart
    and hand,
That calm repose and gallant mien, that courage high
    and grand?—
O God, who givest nations men to meet their lofty
    needs,
Vouchsafe another Thomas when our country prostrate
    bleeds!

They fought with all the fortitude of earnest men and
    true—
The men who wore the rebel gray, the men who wore
    the blue;
And those, they fought most valiantly for petty state and
    clan,
And these, for truer Union and the brotherhood of man.

They come, those hurling legions, with banners crimson
    splashed,
Against our stubborn columns their rushing ranks are
    dashed,
Till 'neath the blistering iron hail the shy and frightened
    deer
Go scurrying from their forest haunts to plunge in
    wilder fear.

Beyond, our lines are broken; and now in frenzied rout
The flower of the Cumberland has swiftly faced about;
And horse and foot and color-guard are reeling rear and
    van,
And in the awful panic man forgets that he is man.

Now Bragg, with pride exultant above our broken wings,
The might of all his army against "Pap" Thomas brings;
They're massing to the right of him, they're massing to
    the left,
Ah, God be with our hero, who holds the crested cleft!

Blow, blow, ye echoing bugles! give answer, screaming
    shell!
Go, belch your murderous fury, ye batteries of hell!
Ring out, O impious musket! spin on, O shattering
    shot,—
Our smoke encircled hero, he hears but heeds ye not!

Now steady, men! now steady! make one more valiant
    stand,
For gallant Steedman's coming, his forces well in hand!
Close up your shattered columns, take steady aim and
    true,
The chief who loves you as his life will live or die with
    you!

By solid columns, on they come; by columns they are
    hurled,
As down the eddying rapids the storm-swept booms are
    whirled;

And when the ammunition fails—O moment drear and
    dread—
The heroes load their blackened guns from rounds of
    soldiers dead.

God never set his signet on the hearts of braver men,
Or fixed the goal of victory on higher heights than then;
With bayonets and muskets clubbed, they close the rush
    and roar;
Their stepping-stones to glory are their comrades gone
    before.

O vanished majesty of days not all forgotten yet,
We consecrate unto thy praise one hour of deep regret;
One hour to them whose days were years of glory that
    shall flood
The Nation's sombre night of tears, of carnage, and of
    blood!

O vanished majesty of days, when men were gauged by
    worth,
Set crowned and dowered in the way to judge the sons
    of earth;
When all the little great fell down before the great
    unknown,
And priest put off the hampering gown and coward
    donned his own!

O vanished majesty of days that saw the sun shine on
The deeds that wake sublimer praise than Ghent or
    Marathon;

When patriots in homespun rose—where one was called
     for, ten—
And heroes sprang full-armored from the humblest
     walks of men!

O vanished majesty of days! Rise, type and mould
     to-day,
And teach our sons to follow on where duty leads the
     way;
That whatsoever trial comes, defying doubt and fear,
They in the thickest fight shall stand and proudly
     answer *"Here!"*

The Dying Words of Stonewall Jackson

"Order A. P. Hill to prepare for battle."
"Tell Major Hawks to advance the Commissary train."
"Let us cross the river and rest in the shade."

The stars of Night contain the glittering Day
And rain his glory down with sweeter grace
Upon the dark World's grand, enchanted face—
    All loth to turn away.

And so the Day, about to yield his breath,
Utters the Stars unto the listening Night,
To stand for burning fare-thee-wells of light
    Said on the verge of death.

O hero-life that lit us like the sun!
O hero-words that glittered like the stars
And stood and shone above the gloomy wars
    When the hero-life was done!

The phantoms of a battle came to dwell
I' the fitful vision of his dying eyes—
Yet even in battle-dreams, he sends supplies
    To those he loved so well.

His army stands in battle-line arrayed:
His couriers fly: all's done: now God decide!
And not till then saw he the Other Side
      Or would accept the shade.

Thou Land whose sun is gone, thy stars remain!
Still shine the words that miniature his deeds.
O thrice-beloved, where'er thy great heart bleeds,
      Solace hast thou for pain!

GEORGIA, September, 1865.

To E. S. Salomon

*Who in a Memorial Day oration protested bitterly against
decorating the graves of Confederate dead.*

What! Salomon! such words from you,
    Who call yourself a soldier? Well,
    The Southern brother where he fell
Slept all your base oration through.

Alike to him—he cannot know
    Your praise or blame: as little harm
    Your tongue can do him as your arm
A quarter-century ago.

The brave respect the brave. The brave
    Respect the dead; but *you*—you draw
    That ancient blade, the ass's jaw,
And shake it o'er a hero's grave.

Are you not he who makes to-day
    A merchandise of old renown
    Which he persuades this easy town
He won in battle far away?

Nay, those the fallen who revile
    Have ne'er before the living stood

And stoutly made their battle good
And greeted danger with a smile.

What if the dead whom still you hate
    Were wrong? Are you so surely right?
    We know the issues of the fight—
The sword is but an advocate.

Men live and die, and other men
    Arise with knowledges diverse:
    What seemed a blessing seems a curse,
And Now is still at odds with Then.

The years go on, the old comes back
    To mock the new—beneath the sun
    Is *nothing* new; ideas run
Recurrent in an endless track.

What most we censure, men as wise
    Have reverently practised; nor
    Will future wisdom fail to war
On principles we dearly prize.

We do not know—we can but deem,
    And he is loyalest and best
    Who takes the light full on his breast
And follows it throughout the dream.

The broken light, the shadows wide—
    Behold the battle-field displayed!
    God save the vanquished from the blade,
The victor from the victor's pride!

If, Salomon, the blessed dew
　　That falls upon the Blue and Gray
　　Is powerless to wash away
The sin of differing from you,

Remember how the flood of years
　　Has rolled across the erring slain;
　　Remember, too, the cleansing rain
Of widows' and of orphans' tears.

The dead are dead—let that atone:
　　And though with equal hand we strew
　　The blooms on saint and sinner too,
Yet God will know to choose his own.

The wretch, whate'er his life and lot,
　　Who does not love the harmless dead
　　With all his heart and all his head—
May God forgive him, *I* shall not.

When, Salomon, you come to quaff
　　The Darker Cup with meeker face,
　　I, loving you at last, shall trace
Upon your tomb this epitaph:

"Draw near, ye generous and brave—
　　Kneel round this monument and weep
　　For one who tried in vain to keep
A flower from a soldier's grave."

A Year's "Casualties"

Slain as they lay by the secret, slow,
Pitiless hand of an unseen foe,
Two score thousand old soldiers have crossed
The river to join the loved and lost.
In the space of a year their spirits fled,
Silent and white, to the camp of the dead.

One after one they fall asleep
And the pension agents awake to weep,
And orphaned statesmen are loud in their wail
As the souls flit by on the evening gale,
O Father of Battles, pray give us release
From the horrors of peace, the horrors of peace!

The Hesitating Veteran

When I was young and full of faith
   And other fads that youngsters cherish
A cry rose as of one that saith
   With emphasis: "Help or I perish!"
'Twas heard in all the land, and men
   The sound were each to each repeating.
It made my heart beat faster then
   Than any heart can now be beating.

For the world is old and the world is gray—
   Grown prudent and, I think, more witty.

She's cut her wisdom teeth, they say,
　　And doesn't now go in for Pity.
Besides, the melancholy cry
　　Was that of one, 'tis now conceded,
Whose plight no one beneath the sky
　　Felt half so poignantly as he did.

Moreover, he was black. And yet
　　That sentimental generation
With an austere compassion set
　　Its face and faith to the occasion.
Then there were hate and strife to spare,
　　And various hard knocks a-plenty;
And I ('twas more than my true share,
　　I must confess) took five-and-twenty.

That all is over now—the reign
　　Of love and trade stills all dissensions,
And the clear heavens arch again
　　Above a land of peace and pensions.
The black chap—at the last we gave
　　Him everything that he had cried for,
Though many white chaps in the grave
　　'Twould puzzle to say what they died for.

I hope he's better off—I trust
　　That his society and his master's
Are worth the price we paid, and must
　　Continue paying, in disasters;
But sometimes doubts press thronging round
　　('Tis mostly when my hurts are aching)

If war for Union was a sound
    And profitable undertaking.

'Tis said they mean to take away
    The Negro's vote for he's unlettered.
'Tis true he sits in darkness day
    And night, as formerly, when fettered;
But pray observe—howe'er he vote
    To whatsoever party turning,
He'll be with gentlemen of note
    And wealth and consequence and learning.

With saints and sages on each side,
    How could a fool through lack of knowledge,
Vote wrong? If learning is no guide
    Why ought one to have been in college?
O Son of Day, O Son of Night!
    What are your preferences made of?
I know not which of you is right,
    Nor which to be the more afraid of.

The world is old and the world is bad,
    And creaks and grinds upon its axis;
And man's an ape and the gods are mad!—
    There's nothing sure, not even our taxes.
No mortal man can Truth restore,
    Or say where she is to be sought for.
I know what uniform I wore—
    O, that I knew which side I fought for!

SOURCES AND
ACKNOWLEDGMENTS

William Cullen Bryant, The Death of Slavery: *Poems* (London: Henry S. King & Co., 1873).

Ralph Waldo Emerson, Boston Hymn: *May-Day and Other Pieces* (Boston. Ticknor & Fields, 1867).

William Gilmore Simms, Ode—"Do Ye Quail?": William Gilmore Simms (ed.), *War Poetry of the South* (New York: Richardson & Co., 1866).

Henry Wadsworth Longfellow, The Witnesses; The Warning; The Cumberland; Killed at the Ford: Horace E. Scudder (ed.), *Works* (Boston: Houghton Mifflin & Co., 1886).

John Greenleaf Whittier, A Word for the Hour; The Battle Autumn of 1862; Anniversary Poem; Barbara Frietchie: *In War Time and Other Poems* (Boston: Ticknor & Fields, 1864). Laus Deo: *National Lyrics* (Boston: Ticknor & Fields, 1865).

Oliver Wendell Holmes, To Canaan: *Songs of Many Seasons 1862–1874* (Boston: James R. Osgood & Co., 1875).

Julia Ward Howe, Battle-Hymn of the Republic: *Later Lyrics* (Boston: J. E. Tilton & Co., 1887).

James Russell Lowell, Ode Recited at the Harvard Commemoration: *Under the Willows and Other Poems* (Boston: Fields, Osgood & Co., 1869).

Herman Melville, The Portent; The March into Virginia; Shiloh; Malvern Hill; The Armies of the Wilderness; The College Colonel; Inscription; A Meditation: *Battle-Pieces and Aspects of the War* (New York: Harper & Brothers, 1866).

Walt Whitman, Cavalry Crossing a Ford; Bivouac on a Mountain Side; The Artilleryman's Vision; Vigil Strange I Kept on the Field One Night; A March in the Ranks Hard-Prest, and the Road Unknown; The Wound-Dresser; Reconciliation; Spirit Whose Work Is Done; O Captain! My Captain!; When Lilacs Last in the Dooryard Bloom'd: *Leaves of Grass* (Philadelphia, 1891–92).

Margaret Junkin Preston, Hymn to the National Flag: William Gilmore Simms (ed.), *War Poetry of the South* (New York: Richardson & Co., 1866). A Grave in Hollywood Cemetery, Richmond: Edmund Clarence Stedman (ed.), *An American Anthology, 1787–1900* (Boston: Houghton Mifflin & Co., 1900).

Henry Howard Brownell, The Bay Fight: *War-Lyrics and Other Poems* (Boston: Ticknor & Fields, 1866)

Thomas Buchanan Read, Sheridan's Ride: *A Summer Story, Sheridan's Ride, and Other Poems* (Philadelphia: J. B. Lippincott, 1865).

Francis Orray Ticknor,; The Virginians of the Valley; Little Giffen: Michelle Cutliff Ticknor (ed.), *The Poems of Francis Orray Ticknor* (New York: Neale, 1911).

George Henry Boker, "Blood, blood! The lines of every printed sheet"; "Oh! craven, craven! while my brothers fall"; Dirge for a Soldier: *Poems of the War* (Boston: Ticknor & Fields, 1864).

Frances Ellen Watkins Harper, The Slave Auction: *Poems on Miscellaneous Subjects* (Boston: J. B. Yerrington & Sons, 1854).

John W. De Forest, from Campaigning; The Storming Column: *Medley and Palestina* (New Haven, CT: Tuttle, Morehouse & Taylor Co., 1902).

Ethel Lynn Beers, All Quiet Along the Potomac: *All Quiet Along the Potomac and Other Poems* (Philadelphia: Porter & Coates, 1879).

Francis Miles Finch, The Blue and the Gray: *Atlantic Monthly*, September 1867.

Henry Timrod, Ethnogenesis; Carolina; Charleston: Unpublished proof sheets, courtesy of the Charleston Library Society, Charleston, South Carolina. Carmen Triumphale; The Unknown Dead: Paul H. Hayne (ed.), *The Poems of Henry Timrod* (New York: E. J. Hale & Son, 1873). Lines: Charleston *Daily Courier*, July 23, 1866.

Fitz-James O'Brien, The Soldier's Letter: William Winter (ed.), *The Poems and Stories of Fitz-James O'Brien* (Boston: J. R. Osgood & Co., 1881).

Silas Weir Mitchell, How the Cumberland Went Down: *The Collected Poems of S. Weir Mitchell* (New York: Century, 1896).

Emily Dickinson, "Of Bronze–and Blaze–"; "If any sink, assure that this, now standing–"; "It feels a shame to be Alive–"; "When I was small, a Woman died–"; "My Portion is Defeat–today–"; "He fought like those Who've nought to lose–": Ralph W. Franklin (ed.), *The Poems of Emily Dickinson*, 3 vols. (Cambridge, Mass.: The Belknap Press of Harvard University Press, 1998).

Paul Hamilton Hayne, Vicksburg—A Ballad: *Poems of Paul Hamilton Hayne* (Boston: D. Lothrop & Co., 1882).

Augusta Cooper Bristol, The Crime of the Ages: *Poems* (Boston: Adams & Co., 1868).

Thomas Bailey Aldrich, Fredericksburg; By the Potomac: *The Works of Thomas Bailey Aldrich* (Boston: Jefferson Press, 1915).

Bret Harte, John Burns of Gettysburg; Relieving Guard: *Poems* (Boston: James R. Osgood & Co., 1871). A Second Review of the Grand Army: *The Poetical Works of Bret Harte* (Household Edition) (Boston: Houghton Mifflin & Co, 1899).

Abram Joseph Ryan, The Sword of Robert Lee: *Poems: Patriotic, Religious, Miscellaneous* (Baltimore, John B. Piet, 1880).

James Ryder Randall, Maryland: New Orleans *Daily Delta*, May 5, 1861.

Nathaniel Southgate Shaler, Near the Front; The Marksman's Work; The Merry Truce: *From Old Fields: Poems of the Civil War* (Boston: Houghton Mifflin & Co., 1906).

Kate Brownlee Sherwood, Thomas at Chickamauga: *Camp-Fire, Memorial Day, and Other Poems* (Chicago: Jansen, McClurg, & Co., 1885).

Sidney Lanier, The Dying Words of Stonewall Jackson: *Poems of Sidney Lanier* (New York: Charles Scribner's Sons, 1904).

Ambrose Bierce, To E. S. Salomon; A Year's "Casualties"; The Hesitating Veteran: *The Collected Works of Ambrose Bierce* (New York: Neale, 1910–1911).

This volume presents the texts of the original printings chosen for inclusion here, but it does not attempt to reproduce nontextual features of their typographic design. The texts are presented without change, except for the correction of typographical errors. Spelling, punctuation, and capitalization are often expressive features and are not altered, even when inconsistent or irregular. The following typographical errors have been corrected (cited by page and line number): 39.11, clings-to; 124.8, Johnson; 158.12, opon.

NOTES

4.2   Boston Hymn]   Emerson recited this poem in Boston's Music Hall on January 1, 1863, the day the Emancipation Proclamation took effect.

9.3   the Beast o'er another Orleans!]   Major General Benjamin F. Butler (1819–1893), the Union military governor of New Orleans from May to December 1862, became known in the Confederacy as "Beast Butler" after he ordered that "any female" who insulted Union soldiers in the city "be treated as a woman of the town plying her avocation."

9.22   Moultrie and Sumter]   Fortresses guarding Charleston harbor.

9.25   the hot spur of Percy]   Cf. Shakespeare, *Henry IV, Part 1*.

13.8   Hampton Roads]   On March 8, 1862, its first day in action, the Confederate ironclad *Virginia* (also known as the *Merrimac*) sank two wooden warships, the *Congress* and the *Cumberland*, commanded by George Upham Morris, and drove the steam frigate *Minnesota* aground in the waters of Hampton Roads, Virginia. The following day the Union ironclad *Monitor* engaged the *Virginia* and forced her to retire up the Elizabeth River.

21.3   Miriam by the sea]   Cf. Exodus 15:20–21.

36.17   VERITAS]   Latin for "truth," and the motto of Harvard University.

43.27   the grapes of Canaan]   See Numbers 13:1–27.

50.2   The Portent]   John Brown and 18 of his followers seized the U.S. armory at Harpers Ferry, Virginia (now West Virginia), on October 16, 1859, with the purpose of arming slaves and starting an insurrection. He was captured on October 18, convicted of treason, and hanged on December 2, 1859.

51.2   *First Manassas*]   Fought in northern Virginia on July 21, 1861, the battle, also known as First Bull Run, ended in a Union rout.

52.9   Second Manassas]   Also known as Second Bull Run, the battle, fought August 29–30, 1862, ended in a Confederate victory.

52.10   Shiloh]   The battle of Shiloh, fought April 6–7, 1862, near Pittsburg Landing, Tennessee, ended in a Union victory. The combined casualties of both armies totaled nearly 24,000 men killed, wounded, or missing.

53.5   Malvern Hill]   The Union army commanded by Major General George B. McClellan repulsed a Confederate attack at Malvern Hill, Virginia, on July 1, 1862.

53.13   the cartridge in their mouth]   Soldiers in the Civil War loaded gunpowder into their rifle muskets by biting open paper cartridges and then pouring the powder down the muzzle.

53.22   Seven Nights and Days]   In the Seven Days' Battles outside Richmond, which began at Oak Grove on June 25 and ended at Malvern Hill, Robert E. Lee succeeded in driving McClellan away from the eastern approaches to the city and caused him to retreat into a defensive position along the James River.

54.16   The Armies of the Wilderness]   The Wilderness, a dense second-growth forest of scrub oak, pine, and underbrush in Spotsylvania County, Virginia, was the scene of two major Civil War battles: the battle of Chancellorsville, May 1–4, 1863, in which Lee succeeded in driving the Union army back across the Rappahannock River, and the battle of the Wilderness, in which Lee attacked the Union army as it moved south through the woods, May 5–6, 1864, but failed to prevent Grant from continuing his southward advance toward Spotsylvania Court House.

57.4   Paran]   Cf. Genesis 21:21.

58.12   Lord Fairfax's parchment deeds]   Thomas, the sixth Lord Fairfax of Cameron (1693–1781), was the proprietor of more than 5 million acres of land between the Rappahannock and the Potomac rivers known as the Northern Neck of Virginia.

59.10   A quiet Man]   Lieutenant General Ulysses S. Grant.

59.26   Mosby's]   Confederate officer John Singleton Mosby (1833–1916) commanded a company of Confederate cavalry raiders who operated behind the Union lines in northern Virginia.

61.11   Stonewall had charged]   Confederate Lieutenant General Thomas (Stonewall) Jackson led a successful attack against the flank of the Union army on May 2, 1863, during the battle of Chancellorsville. He was mortally wounded later that day when his own men mistook his returning scouting party for Union cavalry in the darkness and opened fire.

62.16   Longstreet]   Confederate Lieutenant General James Longstreet led a successful attack against the Union lines in the Wilderness on May 6, 1864, that faltered after he was accidentally wounded by Confederate soldiers.

62.26   Sabæan lore!]   The Sabaeans were the inhabitants of Saba (the Biblical Sheba) in southwest Arabia; their surviving inscriptions have proved difficult to read and interpret.

63.9   The College Colonel]   Inspired by William Francis Bartlett (1840–1876), a Harvard student who was commissioned as a captain in a Massachusetts regiment in 1861. He lost a leg in the Peninsula Campaign in 1862, but remained in the army and organized a new regiment. Bartlett was wounded again at Port Hudson and in the Wilderness. He was wounded and captured in the Petersburg mine crater battle on July 30, 1864, and held in Libby Prison in Richmond.

64.18   *Marye's Heights, Fredericksburg*]   During the battle of Fredericksburg, December 13, 1862, the Union Army of the Potomac crossed the Rappahannock River and unsuccessfully attacked Marye's Heights. The battle ended in a Confederate victory and the loss of nearly 13,000 Union soldiers killed or wounded.

66.10   fields in Mexico]   Many of the officers who fought on opposing sides in the Civil War had served together during the Mexican War, 1846–48.

66.25   on the Hudson's marge]   At West Point.

67.13   When Vicksburg fell]   On July 4, 1863, the city surrendered after a siege of 43 days.

96.2   (*J.R.T.*)]   John Reuben Thompson (1823–1873) was a poet and the editor of the *Southern Literary Messenger* from 1847 to 1860. Thompson lived in England, 1864–66, before becoming literary editor of the New York *Evening Post.* He died in New York and was buried in Hollywood Cemetery in Richmond.

97.9–11   the Poet . . . Bold Stuart]   Thompson wrote several poems about the Civil War, including "Obsequies of Stuart (May 12, 1864)." Confederate cavalry commander Major General J.E.B. Stuart was wounded at Yellow Tavern, Virginia, on May 11, 1864, and died in Richmond the following day.

98.2   The Bay Fight]   On August 5, 1864, Rear Admiral David G. Farragut led a Union fleet of four ironclad monitors and 14 wooden steamships into Mobile Bay. Brownell, who was serving as Farragut's secretary, witnessed the battle from the U.S.S. *Hartford*, the Union flagship.

99.16   Lion-Heart]   Richard I (1157–1199), king of England, called "Coeur de Lion," a leader of the Third Crusade in 1189–92.

100.10   Kimberly]   Lieutenant Commander Lewis Kimberly, executive officer of the *Hartford*.

100.17–18   Gaines . . . Morgan]   Confederate forts guarding the entrance to the bay.

100.25   River-Wars]   The *Hartford* had fought at New Orleans, Vicksburg, and Port Hudson, 1862–63.

102.13–14   Dahlgren, / Parrott, and Sawyer]   Types of rifled cannon used by the Union navy.

103.2   Craven]   Captain Tunis Craven, who was lost along with 92 of his crew when the monitor *Tecumseh* struck a torpedo (floating mine) and sank.

103.27   the Tennessee]   The C.S.S. *Tennessee*, a large ironclad ram.

108.25   Jouett]   Lieutenant Commander James E. Jouett, commander of the U.S.S. *Metacomet*, a wooden steamship that entered the bay lashed to the *Hartford*. She subsequently cut herself loose and captured the Confederate gunboat *Selma*.

109.17   Philippi]   A Union gunboat that had attempted to follow the fleet into the bay.

110.12   Our Monitors]   The *Winnebago*, *Manhattan*, and *Chickasaw*.

110.17–22   Monongahela . . . Lackawana]   Wooden steamships in the Union fleet.

111.13   Drayton]   Captain Percival Drayton, commander of the *Hartford*.

113.4   Marchand]   Captain J. B. Marchand, commander of the *Lackawanna*.

113.5   brave Strong]   Commander James H. Strong, captain of the *Monongahela*.

113.23   He sank in the Cumberland]   Franklin Buchanan (1800–1874), the commander of the Confederate fleet at Mobile Bay, had been captain of the ironclad *Virginia* in March 1862; see note 13.8.

119.2   Sheridan's Ride]   At dawn on October 19, 1864, Confederate troops under Lieutenant General Jubal A. Early surprised Union forces at Cedar Creek, Virginia, and drove them from their positions. Major General Philip Henry Sheridan, who was returning to his command from a conference in Washington, learned of the attack in Winchester, Virginia, and rode to the front on his horse Rienzi, rallying stragglers and directing a successful counterattack.

122.10   Spotswood]   Alexander Spotswood (1676–1740) was the lieutenant governor (de facto governor) of Virginia from 1710 to 1722.

123.1   the "Golden Horseshoe" Knights]   Spotswood presented golden
horseshoe-shaped pins to his companions on his 1716 expedition across
the Blue Ridge Mountains.

124.8   Johnston]   Confederate General Joseph E. Johnston (1807–
1891).

124.15   knights of the Golden Ring]   A pro-slavery secret society
formed in the 1850s, also known as the Knights of the Golden Circle.

126.8   *General Philip Kearny*]   Union Major General Philip Kearny
(1814–1862) was killed in action at Chantilly, Virginia, on September 1,
1862. Kearny had lost his left arm during the Mexican War and had also
fought with the French in Italy in 1859.

130.19   Banks]   Major General Nathaniel P. Banks ordered assaults on
the Confederate lines at Port Hudson, Louisiana, on June 11 and 14,
1863.

138.2   Ethnogenesis]   The genesis or beginnings of a race. The Southern Congress (or Convention) in Montgomery, Alabama, was attended
by delegates from South Carolina, Georgia, Florida, Alabama, Mississippi, and Louisiana; they met on February 4, 1861, adopted a provisional constitution for the Confederate States of America, and unani-
mously elected Jefferson Davis as provisional president.

139.22   Moultrie and of Eutaw]   Colonel William Moultrie built a fort
on Sullivan's Island off Charleston, South Carolina, and successfully de-
fended it against a British naval attack on June 28, 1776; it was later
named after him. The battle of Eutaw Springs, South Carolina, fought
on September 8, 1781, ended with the British forces retreating to
Charleston and abandoning their attempts to hold outposts in the inte-
rior of the state.

143.8   How Rutledge ruled and Laurens died]   John Rutledge (1739–
1800) was president of the South Carolina general assembly, 1776–78,
and governor of South Carolina, 1779–82; as governor he helped organ-
ize resistance to the British occupation. Lieutenant Colonel John Laurens (1724–1782), the son of South Carolina statesman Henry Laurens,
was killed in a skirmish at Combahee, South Carolina, in 1782.

143.11   Marion's bugle blast]   Francis Marion (1732?–1795), known as
"the Swamp Fox," led partisans against British forces in South Carolina.

145.17   Calpe]   The ancient name for the Rock of Gibralter.

151.1   Lines]   The poem was sung on June 16, 1866, at a grave decora-
tion ceremony for the Confederate dead at Magnolia Cemetery in
Charleston, South Carolina.

158.20   none but Daisies, know –]   The text printed here is taken from *The Poems of Emily Dickinson*, edited by R. W. Franklin (3 vols., 1998). An earlier edition, *The Complete Poems of Emily Dickinson*, edited by Thomas H. Johnson (1960), printed a variant reading: "none but Beetles – know."

169.2   John Burns of Gettysburg]   John Burns (c.1791–1872), a veteran of the War of 1812 and a resident of Gettysburg, joined the Union forces as the battle began on July 1, 1863, and was wounded during the fighting.

169.16   a stubborn Meade]   Major General George G. Meade (1815–1872), the Union commander at Gettysburg.

172.15   crested plume of the brave Navarre}   Henry of Navarre (1553–1610) wore a white plume on his helmet while in battle.

173.2   T.S.K.]   Thomas Starr King (1824–1864) was a Unitarian minister who moved from Boston to San Francisco in 1860. A popular orator, King campaigned for Lincoln and in 1861 rallied support for the Union throughout California. He then became a successful fundraiser for the U.S. Sanitary Commission before dying from diphtheria and pneumonia.

173.16   the grand review]   The "Grand Review" of the Union armies of the Potomac, the Tennessee, and Georgia was held in Washington, D.C., May 23–24, 1865.

175.16   dusky martyrs of Pillow's fight]   After capturing Fort Pillow in Tennessee on April 12, 1864, Confederate cavalrymen killed several dozen black soldiers.

179.7–8   patriotic gore . . . Baltimore]   Twelve citizens of Baltimore were killed by soldiers of the 6th Massachusetts Regiment on April 19, 1861, after a pro-secessionist mob had attacked the regiment as it marched through the city.

179.23   Carroll's sacred trust]   Charles Carroll of Carrollton (1736–1832), a signer of the Declaration of Independence.

179.24   Howard's warlike thrust]   John Eager Howard (1752–1827), an officer in the Continental army who fought in eight major battles during the Revolutionary War and was severely wounded at Eutaw Springs. He later served as governor of Maryland, 1789–91, and as a senator, 1796–1803.

180.7   Ringgold's spirit]   Major Samuel Ringgold (1800–1846), an army officer from Maryland who fought the Seminoles in Florida and was mortally wounded on May 8, 1846, at the battle of Palo Alto.

180.8   Watson's blood]   Lieutenant Colonel William Watson (1808–1846), the commander of the Baltimore Battalion in the Mexican War, was killed on September 21, 1846, during the American attack on Monterrey.

180.9   fearless Lowe and dashing May]   Enoch Lewis Lowe (1820–1892) was the Democratic governor of Maryland, 1851–54, and a supporter of the Confederacy during the Civil War, which he spent in the South. Captain Charles A. May (1819–1864) became famous for leading a charge of dragoons against Mexican artillery at the battle of Resaca de la Palma on May 9, 1846. May resigned from the army in 1861 and did not serve during the Civil War.

180.17   a new *Key*]   Francis Scott Key (1779–1843), who wrote "Defence of Fort McHenry" after witnessing the British bombardment of the Baltimore harbor defenses on September 13–14, 1814; the poem was set to music as "The Star-Spangled Banner."

180.24   "*Sic semper*,"]   In full, *sic semper tyrannis*, "thus always to tyrants," the motto of Virginia.

181.19   The Old Line's bugle]   "The Old Line" was a name for the Maryland regiments of the Continental army during the Revolutionary War.

188.2   Thomas at Chickamauga]   On the second day of the battle of Chickamauga, fought in northwestern Georgia, September 19–20, 1863, Confederate troops found a gap in the Union lines and routed the right wing of the Army of the Cumberland. While Major General William S. Rosecrans, the army's commander, and other senior Union officers fled with their troops toward Chattanooga, Major General George H. Thomas (1816–1870), the commander of the XIV Corps, formed a new horseshoe-shaped line that held for the remainder of the day and prevented a complete rout of the Union forces. Thomas became known as "the Rock of Chickamauga."

188.9   *Harker*]   Charles G. Harker (1837–1864) commanded a Union brigade at Chickamauga and was later killed in action at Kennesaw Mountain, Georgia.

190.6   Bragg]   General Braxton Bragg (1817–1876) commanded the Confederate Army of Tennessee at Chickamauga. He resigned his command shortly after his defeat in the battle of Chattanooga, November 23–25, 1863.

190.19   Steedman's]   Brigadier General James B. Steedman (1817–1883), the commander of a Union division at Chickamauga, reinforced Thomas at a crucial point in the battle and then led a successful counterattack.

191.26   Ghent]   A revolt in Ghent in 1577 against Spanish rule resulted in the establishment of a Calvinist republic that lasted until the Spanish capture of the city in 1584.

191.27   Marathon]   The Athenians defeated the invading Persian army at Marathon in 490 B.C.

193.2   The Dying Words of Jackson]   Confederate Lieutenant General Thomas J. (Stonewall) Jackson was accidentally shot by his own men during the battle of Chancellorsville on May 2, 1863, and died of pneumonia eight days later. He spoke the words in the epigraph in his final delirium.

195.2   E. S. Salomon]   Edward S. Salomon (1836–1913), a German immigrant, commanded an Illinois volunteer regiment during the war. He later served as governor of Washington Territory, 1870–72, and in the California assembly, 1889–91.

198.1   A Year's "Casualties"]   The poem first appeared in the *San Francisco Examiner* on December 28, 1890.

AMERICAN POETS PROJECT

1. **EDNA ST. VINCENT MILLAY** / J. D. McClatchy, editor

2. **POETS OF WORLD WAR II** / Harvey Shapiro, editor

3. **KARL SHAPIRO** / John Updike, editor

4. **WALT WHITMAN** / Harold Bloom, editor

5. **EDGAR ALLAN POE** / Richard Wilbur, editor

6. **YVOR WINTERS** / Thom Gunn, editor

7. **AMERICAN WITS** / John Hollander, editor

8. **KENNETH FEARING** / Robert Polito, editor

9. **MURIEL RUKEYSER** / Adrienne Rich, editor

10. **JOHN GREENLEAF WHITTIER** / Brenda Wineapple, editor

11. **JOHN BERRYMAN** / Kevin Young, editor

12. **AMY LOWELL** / Honor Moore, editor

13. **WILLIAM CARLOS WILLIAMS** / Robert Pinsky, editor

14. **POETS OF THE CIVIL WAR** / J. D. McClatchy, editor

15. **THEODORE ROETHKE** / Edward Hirsch, editor

16. **EMMA LAZARUS** / John Hollander, editor